NECESSARY
LESSONS

NECESSARY LESSONS

Decline and Renewal in American Schools

GILBERT T. SEWALL

THE FREE PRESS
A Division of Macmillan, Inc.
NEW YORK
Collier Macmillan Publishers
LONDON

The Free Press
A Division of Macmillan, Inc.
866 Third Avenue, New York, N.Y. 10022

Collier Macmillan Canada, Inc.

Printed in the United States of America

printing number

1 2 3 4 5 6 7 8 9 10

Library of Congress Cataloging in Publication Data

Sewall, Gilbert T.
    Necessary lessons.

    Bibliography: p.
    Includes index.
    1. Education, Secondary—United States—Philosophy.
2. Progressive education—United States.   3. Education,
Secondary—United States—Aims and objectives.   4. Educational sociology—United States.   I. Title.
LA222.S46   1983   373.73   83–47980
    ISBN 0–02–929030–9

*For
Jean and my family,
with special debts to Checker*

Contents

Preface

It was a damp and gray January afternoon in 1980. I sat back in the yellow cab and tried to collect my thoughts. My destination was Teachers College at Columbia University. As education editor at *Newsweek,* I had been following the breaking news and trends in education, especially at the high school level, with increasing alarm. After fifteen years of the most ambitious elementary and secondary school reform ventures ever, almost any accurate student profile for youth of any background, ability, or region indicated qualitative decline. Especially in municipal public schools, it seemed, a complex of legal, regulatory, and customary initiatives—wearing the plumage of "reform"—was carrying public schools toward a possible point of no return.

The car slid to a halt in front of the red brick complex of Victorian buildings and Gothic portals. (Over the doorway, cut into Connecticut brownstone: MENS SANA IN CORPORE SANO.) I paid the driver and walked toward the president's office. Moments later Lawrence Cremin received me graciously. I had come to ask his advice about an article I was then preparing. President Cremin, this country's acknowledged master of educational scholarship, at that time had just completed the second volume of his definitive history of U.S. education, later to win a Pulitzer Prize. In a brilliant and patrician style, Cremin began to explain the situation with clarity and force.

Cremin admitted that *some* schools were in terrible shape. "But society gets what it deserves," he said. "With the decline of the family and church, schools have had to assume new responsibilities of socialization. They must deal with the potential killer or the kid headed for the subterranean economy. There is no longer the 'school' of the field and workplace, which is where most children were once educated." Yet Cremin did not share my despondent mood. He rejected crisply my contention that in places the public school system would break down in the eighties. "You're in danger of writing the last education story of the seventies," he said. "Why not come into this decade?"

According to Cremin, the truly interesting news of the eighties was growing curiosity about and understanding of what he called instructionally effective schools. "The future is not with private schools," he said. "It is with those schools that stress an old-time curriculum, decent values, security, and order. That's the story you should tell."

⌒

I have tried to. Since then I have traveled to some thirty elementary and secondary schools in California, Connecticut, Illinois, Michigan, New Jersey, New York, North Carolina, and Pennsylvania. The point of these visits has been not to conduct a systematic survey but to observe and interview, to sharpen my image of school people and students, to record the ethos of public and private schooling in the early eighties. There have been a hundred surprises.

Uncovering a world of anomalies and contradictions, I have become ever more wary of generalizations about schools that I used to make without much thought. I have reflected on biases collected during eight years of high school teaching. I have seen firsthand the store of effort, goodwill, and selflessness—especially among teachers—that everywhere is part of the educational enterprise. Where failure is conspicuous, too, I have grown accustomed to administrative dread of reporters and the system's cynical defense of current conditions. A young and ambitious Greenwich, Connecticut, principal put it this way: "There hasn't been a book that has helped education in the last ten years," he said. When I challenged that remark, he corrected himself. "Rather, there hasn't been a book to help the public image of school." Then he said curtly, "It is not in my interest to help you." Since I had gone to Greenwich in the first place to observe an outstanding suburban high school, that was my first tipoff that the local system might not be all it was cracked up to be. (Most school observers have private barometers that help them to gauge quality. For some, it is the state of the lavatories. For me, how enthusiastically a school's students and administrators greet outsiders is as good an index.)

While I amassed the freshest and most reliable data available, collected reports, conducted interviews, and read news bulletins, I became more and more astonished by what may be called the "good news syndrome." True, the schools have been besieged by negative press during the last few years. Too often their ample successes have been ignored. But many educators—benefiting from current conditions—resent all unfavorable analysis, acting as though what they do should be beyond public criticism. Increasingly, they are growing annoyed with and afraid of restive clients who reject the idea that U.S. schools have never been better. A 1980 issue of *The American School Board Journal,* for example, belligerently advised its readers to "blast your critics with education's good news." It published a list of facts designed to silence adversaries, such as, "In science, U.S. students are doing better than students in Britain, the Netherlands, and Italy." Presumably to raise one's hand and ask about comparisons with Germany, Japan, and the Soviet Union would be in the poorest of taste.

In the first section of this book I review the historical conditions, philosophic currents, political impulses, and short-run trends that gave rise to the disagreeable state of schooling on the day I went to visit President Cremin. The second section explores current reform initiatives, research on instructionally effective schools, and the meaning of basic education. In this part I make prescriptive recommendations for the eighties and beyond. The purpose of both parts is to engender debate on what practices and aims reformers might pursue to stimulate educational quality.

The nation is embarking on a critical period in its educational history. It is about time. More than most school observers, I believe that the record of public education during the last dozen or so years is on balance a sorry one. And too often, in spite of the ostentatious compassion of liberal reformers, the real losers during the sixties and seventies were disadvantaged youth, given unprecedented educational opportunities with one hand as the other hand snatched away serious scholastic and behavioral standards. In a complex society such as ours, the presence of uneducated, unskilled, and dependent citizens imperils national security and exacts a huge toll in human suffering. If the new reformers are successful, schools will come closer to realizing the authentic democratic ideal of sound mass education, a concept that has had much lip service over the last century but, to date, a goal that has remained elusive.

With enormous pleasure I state my gratitude to the many kind individuals and institutions that have assisted me during the preparation of this manuscript. First, I thank its sponsor. The project originated in an invitation in the fall of 1980 by the Council for Basic Education to write a report on and case for subject-centered school reform. I am grateful to the Council for its sufficient trust to make all matters of content rest wholly and fully in my hands. I was fortunate, too, to have spent a year as a research associate at Teachers College's Institute for Philosophy and Politics of Education, completing the research phase of the book with financial support from the Council for Basic Education, the Institute for Educational Affairs, and the Exxon Education Foundation.

The book was written almost entirely during the year of residence at the National Humanities Center during 1981–82. The Center was an idyllic place to work, a splendid research center tucked in the North Carolina pine forests outside of Chapel Hill. There I was blessed by the company of stimulating colleagues, the unfailing kindness of the staff, and the valiant work of Karen Carroll as chief manuscript typist. At critical moments during the project I was assisted and encouraged by William Bennett, Steven Cahn, Dennis Gray, Diane Ravitch, and Theodore Sizer. Without them, and others, tackling and completing the book would have been impossible. I thank all of these wise scholars for their help and for showing me by example what educational excellence means.

G. T. S.

New York, New York
January 1983

NECESSARY LESSONS

ONE

A Report Card

A FEW MINUTES AFTER NINE the buzzer rings. "Today's class is going to be about westward expansion," the gray-haired teacher tells her twelfth-grade social studies class. But engrossed in their own conversations, the two dozen students ignore her. One boy baas like a sheep, and some youngsters laugh. Others stare out the window or nestle in their chairs to sleep. To the handful of serious students trying to follow her jumbled lecture and audio-visual presentation, the Louisiana Purchase and Mexican War seem to have taken place in the same decade. It is painfully clear that the teacher neither knows her subject nor has the personality to make the lesson interesting. Ten minutes later the door bursts open. Several youngsters, smirking at their tardiness, saunter into class. One girl interrupts the teacher to demand a pencil and piece of paper. By now the class is so confused that even the most stalwart students close their notebooks and give up. Says one hulking student loudly, "This stuff really sucks." The teacher flinches, her eyes look tired and frightened, but she says nothing. Her day is just beginning.

This is Pittsburgh's Carrick High School, perched on a windswept

1

hill two miles southeast of the confluence of the Allegheny and Monongahela rivers. In 1980, 85 percent of its student body was white, the scions of ethnically conscious Irish, Polish, and Italian parents whose family incomes averaged something around $17,000 annually. A quarter of its graduates matriculated at four-year colleges; the rest searched for factory jobs, went to trade schools or community colleges, or entered the army. Carrick was a safe school, the only one of Pittsburgh's twelve "inner-city" high schools still to hold evening dances. The school had a handful of truly gifted teachers, an earnest and able principal, a clean and well-supplied physical plant. Its blue-collar parents chafed at a citywide desegregation plan that threatened their white enclave. But they showed no signs of deserting the school in short order on account of "the race problem." Carrick was not an all-purpose social service and custodial center for children from welfare-dependent families. Nor was it a suburban garden campus for the offspring of wealthy executives.

Carrick was pertinent because it operated not far from the middle of the U.S. public high school's spectrum of quality. And its pathetic second-period social studies class was instructive: A perfectly acceptable history syllabus had been poisoned by an inept, abused, worn-out teacher and ill-mannered, hostile students. Unlike many thousands of other schools across the country in 1980, Carrick was not "in trouble." Yet on a typical day a large portion of its students dozed through their classes; scuffles broke out in classrooms; teenage drug dealers openly sold their wares at a nearby delicatessen; and a cafeteria worker complained that an emotionally disturbed student had recently threatened her with a knife. Almost two hundred pupils, or 10 percent of the student body, were truant. Many more cut individual classes. "Too many kids here simply don't care," said the principal Jack Palmer. "We adults have given them the message that they don't need to work or learn."

Was Mr. Palmer's assertion correct? Too sweeping? Alarmist? Were large numbers of American students, left rudderless by the erosion of adult guidance and authority, throwing in the towel at an early age? At the dawn of a new decade, was a widely perceived failure

2

of the schools to prepare the young for either advanced education or effective participation in democratic culture imagined or real?

No one could agree. Defensive educational leaders claimed that schools were merely victims of bad press and overblown expectations. Many school analysts acknowledged glaring institutional deficiencies but cited complex and disturbing social forces to explain why present conditions were the best one could hope for realistically. School critics demanded change. Some activists called for extensive public programs to promote juvenile justice and welfare. Other reformers wanted to abandon many existing school practices and substitute more academically centered programs. Diagnoses varied. Yet to just about everyone who had no vested interest in maintaining schooling's status quo, something was dreadfully wrong.

Consider the evidence. Although virtually all adult Americans, except for the retarded, can read and write at the Dick-and-Jane level, a disturbing number of them are unable to employ words with enough skill to understand directions, perform simple jobs, or read a newspaper. The incidence is especially high for nonwhites. In 1982 the Department of Defense released results of a survey to determine U.S. manpower capabilities based on a representative national sample of nearly 12,000 eighteen- to twenty-three-year-olds. On this test of basic verbal and mathematical skills, average achievement scores of whites were more than double those of blacks. According to a 1979 report prepared for Senator George McGovern, based in part on the findings of the National Assessment of Educational Progress, the number of seventeen-year-old "functional illiterates" is perhaps as high as 13 percent of whites, rising to a harrowing 42 percent of blacks and 56 percent of Hispanics.

For at least 23 million adult Americans, the instructions in a laundromat are mystifying; reading a repair manual or filling out a job application accurately is impossible. Bluntly stated, these citizens do not have the survival skills to compete in a highly specialized service economy that values, above all, mental agility and reliability. Consequently they have little or no stake in the future of democratic capitalism. These functional illiterates are condemned to live on the fringe of the polity as menial laborers, as welfare recipients, as outlaws, as the emotionally tortured and spiritually broken. Doomed to inse-

3

cure, insolvent, and possibly violent futures, they are what society considers failed people. True, most middle-class children grow up to be functionally literate. But will that literacy be inert or liberating? The answer depends in large part on the store of knowledge and reasoning ability they carry away from school. Thus, average student outcomes today may be one useful index of citizen initiative in the future.

Since 1969 the National Assessment of Educational Progress has monitored certain educational achievements of American youth. The federally financed survey was once controversial: Critics feared, incorrectly, that the NAEP would become a national testing program used to make invidious comparisons between schools, school systems, and states. But today a continuing assessment in major learning areas tests the knowledge, skills, understanding, and attitudes of nine-, thirteen-, and seventeen-year-olds. It is the nation's most sensitive means of gauging student, group, and regional attainments from the fourth through the twelfth grade.

Through surveys conducted between 1970 and 1981 the NAEP revealed several trends:*

- Academic troubles usually started in fifth or sixth grade and intensified through high school. In junior and senior high schools, achievement in virtually all basic subjects and skills atrophied during this period. In the elementary schools, significantly, educational performance remained relatively steady and, in the case of reading, improved substantially.
- Achievement in abstract problem-solving and reasoning plunged dramatically. After 1973 the ability to compute—to add, subtract, multiply, and divide—did not decline, a 1978 mathematics assessment showed. What slipped was the ability

* Presented with a caveat: 1969 and 1970, base years for calculating changes in educational achievement, were years of low student attainments and considerable schoolyard tumult. Major standardized examinations from the Scholastic Aptitude Test to the Iowa Test of Basic Skills recorded substantial academic improvement at the national level from 1958 to 1963, followed by a period of declining student performance. The declines recorded here, then, are not the fall from a "golden age." It was in response to early concern over alleged declines in student achievement and to what U.S. Education Commissioner Francis Keppel called "a woeful shortage of basic knowledge about how much our children really know" that the NAEP was established.

for students of all age levels to think through problems, to understand a given set of facts and apply mathematical solutions. Similarly, a review of reading assessments from 1970 to 1980 showed declines for thirteen- and seventeen-year-olds in "inferential comprehension," the skill that enables students to draw conclusions, form judgments, and create new ideas. In addition, some students who did well on NAEP multiple choice tests—and thus received high scores—could not formulate their ideas in sentences and paragraphs. To NAEP researchers, all these findings indicated that the core of the learning crisis was not declining performance in the basic skills. It was, instead, the failure of students to master the higher faculties of analysis and critical thinking.

- Student knowledge of the structure and function of government declined sharply. In 1976, for instance, only 42 percent of eighth-graders could explain the basic meaning of "democracy"; 36 percent of twelfth-graders understood how presidential candidates are selected. Four years earlier more than half of each group taking the test could answer the same questions correctly.
- Between 1969 and 1974 the coherence and quality of student writing deteriorated. In the later seventies, partly on account of public distress at NAEP findings and subsequent media attacks on injury to the language, grammar and composition enjoyed renewed emphasis among English instructors.
- Time spent doing homework declined. By 1978 over two-thirds of high school seniors spent less than five hours per week doing homework. Only 6 percent spent more than ten hours. Not surprisingly, those students who did the most homework and watched the least television scored the highest on NAEP tests.
- A steady decline in science achievement occurred among 17-year-olds.

Besides this, to the special horror of college-educated parents and national publications, which gave the phenomenon extraordinary attention, student performance softened at the top. The College Board's Scholastic Aptitude Test, a consistent benchmark of mathematical and verbal abilities of college-bound students since the fifties, registered steady slippage: Median verbal scores on a scale from 200 to 800 plummeted from a high of 478 in 1963 to a low of 424 in 1980; in the same period mathematics scores fell from 502 to 466. Some attributed this decline to increasing numbers of minorities, females, and low-income students taking the test. But no. After 1970 the composition of SAT-takers remained quite stable, and since then the drops have been most extensive. According to a critical review of nine major testing programs conducted by researchers Annegret Harnischfeger and David E. Wiley in 1975,* these SAT trends were not aberrant: In almost all examinations average scores began to tumble about 1965, most precipitously in the higher grades, and in verbal areas.

For youngsters of all backgrounds and capabilities, academic outcomes are low and, at least until very recently, have been shrinking. Why? To begin with, few pupils at the secondary level are required to take courses in all the basic subjects—language, math, history, science—in order to qualify for a high school diploma. Only about 34 percent of public high school students today pursue an academic course of study rather than a general or vocational program, even though more than half go on to college. Roughly 85 percent take no foreign language; 63 percent, no chemistry; 47 percent, no geometry; 20 percent, no science whatsoever. In the eleventh and twelfth grades, half of the students take no math or science, and 27 percent take no English.

Even more disturbing, curricular revisions have steadily diluted course content. New syllabuses in basic subjects have appeared, purged of tedious or difficult units. Vacuous electives have proliferated, allowing some students to sidestep challenging courses altogether (nonetheless satisfying diploma requirements). Students who do decide to take upper-level English courses might have the chance to choose courses *for equal credit* in journalism, science fiction, filmmaking, Shakespeare, or expository writing. Social studies classes might substitute trendy units in human rights, the limits of growth, or nuclear disarmament for map-reading exercises or the study of the Civil War. A civics requirement might be satisfied by a course that focuses on the constitu-

* See "References" section following Chapter Ten for fuller citations of sources by chapter.

tional protections that every citizen is guaranteed but has little to say about the Bill of Rights' relation to public responsibilities. In some extreme cases citizenship training simply stops, replaced by values education programs in which students spend class time "clarifying" what viewpoints and activities each of them likes or dislikes, with all outlooks taken as equally valid. Endless courses in family life, personal adjustment, consumer skills, and business have crowded out more rigorous subjects, notably in science and foreign language.

While the curriculum has been debased, grades have gone up. Honor grades of "B" and "A" no longer signify above-average or outstanding work. Many teachers believe that it is more "caring" to evaluate students on the basis of effort or improvement rather than against some common standard. Some teachers shy away from giving low grades that could hurt their students' chances of graduation or of college admission. Other teachers, often poorly educated themselves, are unable to discriminate between superior and mediocre work. Sometimes tacit pressure exists to assess minority students more generously than white students: Shivering at the prospect of being called racist, some teachers are unable to hold nonwhite youngsters to strict academic account. As a result of all of this, any teacher with exacting standards runs the risk of interference from students, parents, administrators, and colleagues, all of them ready to challenge the instructor's informed opinion. Not surprisingly, as more teachers withdraw from their traditional positions as standard-setters for a younger generation, many students grasp the fact that they have the power to defy, circumvent, or ignore adults in schools.

What this last phenomenon amounts to is a crisis of authority. And that crisis appears even more virulent outside the classroom than within it. To some worried parents, academic inadequacy pales beside the apparent breakdown of schoolhouse order. After ten years or more they still remember the early warning signals in urban high schools with shock: lunchrooms and hallways turning into battlegrounds of black and white, graffiti sprayed on old Palladian columns, security guards with walkie-talkies patrolling corridors, bathrooms harboring dope smokers. Many have watched the plague of antisocial and self-destructive behavior spread to suburban and rural communities. In-

7

most cases conditions have stabilized; at least school crime is not getting worse.* But nowadays parents have stopped hoping that symptoms of the authority crisis will disappear like a bad dream.

Today the attitude problems remain: backtalk, blaring radios, wastepaper baskets set on fire. Disobedience sometimes slides into sociopathic and criminal behavior: the torture of classroom pets or lab animals, the smashing of expensive audio-visual equipment, bomb threats. In some schools a lawless student subculture is large and brazen enough to demoralize an entire student body. Much insult is directed at teachers: slashed tires, sexual humiliation, occasionally murder. In a 1979 press release, the National Education Association estimated that during the previous school year 110,000 teachers had been assaulted by young people in school. To parents and others who were graduated from high school before 1965, such hateful acts strain credulity. By comparison the delinquents who inhabited the "blackboard jungle" of the fifties seem almost wholesome.

In response to early—"anecdotal"—reports of chronic violence in public schools, not just in the central cities but all over the country, Congress sponsored a survey to determine its seriousness and extent. The study dealt only with disruptive and criminal acts, not with self-destructive behavior. Between 1974 and 1977 researchers queried more than 4,000 schools, 31,000 students, and 23,000 teachers. Then 6,000 student respondents were selected for face-to-face interviews. In January 1978 the National Institute of Education published a 350-page report called *Violent Schools—Safe Schools.*

Its findings confirmed some dark suspicions:

- The crime problem was most acute at the junior high school level. In urban intermediate schools, 8.2 percent of students reported being physically attacked in the previous month, compared with 3 percent of suburban high school students.

---

* This is in part the outcome of newer trends: soaring truancy and dropout rates. In many big-city school systems, school attendance laws have simply broken down. High school dropout rates in downtown areas are staggering: according to one 1982 estimate, nearly 70 percent in Detroit, 56 percent in Chicago, 48 percent in Boston, and 44 percent in New York. Since truants and potential dropouts are most likely to be troublemakers, few school administrators still try to keep adolescents in school against their will.

- About 8 percent of the nation's schools had "serious" crime problems. Assaults and robberies were most prevalent in inner-city secondary schools where most students were black and Hispanic, came from low-income families, and performed at low academic levels. Most crimes involved victims and offenders of the same race, but fully 42 percent of the assaults and 46 percent of reported robberies were interracial.
- An incredible 2.4 million thefts of personal property occurred at schools each month. The cost of replacing damaged or stolen school property was at least $200 million each year.
- More than half of big-city junior high schools and two-thirds of big-city senior high schools had trained security personnel to police corridors and campuses.
- Twenty percent of all students were at least sometimes afraid of being hurt or bothered at school.
- Contrary to conventional wisdom, students, not juvenile intruders, were responsible for most school crime.

Later, in a penetrating analysis of the report for *The Public Interest* magazine, the Rutgers sociologist Jackson Toby explained how concerned parents avoided unsafe schools. "For families with the economic means to do so," he said, "the easiest way was to transfer their children to private or parochial schools or to move to suburban communities with reputations for good schools." Poorer families were stuck: They could afford neither private school tuitions nor houses in communities with superior schools. As a result, Toby concluded, "as crime grew more serious in big-city schools, they became less and less functional as a channel of social ascent for able students from disadvantaged backgrounds; they became traps instead of springboards."

In resources and products, U.S. schools vary enormously. Substantial community control distinguishes them from the highly centralized educational systems of all other advanced industrial countries. In spite of extensive federal and state activity in schools today, they remain the most local institution in America. About 16,000 separate governing boards oversee the operations of their individual school districts. The average district is 2,600 students in size. But these units range from the vast metropolitan systems of Los Angeles or Miami to tiny one-school districts in Vermont or eastern Montana, where school principal and superintendent are one and the same. Such differences also apply to school finances: Colorado obtains about 6 percent of its school revenues from Washington, while Mississippi receives more than 17 percent of its revenues from the federal government. Generalizations about school quality are likewise risky. New York's selective inner-city Stuyvesant High School sends dozens of its graduates to the Ivy League each year; at Philadelphia's Edison High, a majority of the student body reads at third-grade level or below. The public schools of tax-rich Darien, Connecticut, and impoverished Newark, New Jersey, inhabit different social universes, though they lie only 35 miles apart. Private schools vary too: from parklike suburban day schools where Advanced Placement courses are the rule, to no-nonsense urban parochial schools, to rough-hewn tabernacle schools in rural church basements.

Still, in the midst of this diversity, it is not incorrect to recognize a pervasive force that guides national school policies. In the United States public education has long been dominated by an army of administrators, planners, researchers, and other experts that culminates in the elite corps called the "education establishment." At any moment certain assumptions about the way schools should work emanate from this well-intentioned leadership. Inevitably, and in most cases unofficially, shared attitudes at the top trickle down into the classroom practices, platitudes, and public statements of local educators.

For the last generation this heterogeneous, sometimes truculent establishment has subscribed to an essentially secular, egalitarian, and socially prescriptive view of schooling. Accordingly, its views have come to rest in the marrow of "autonomous" school districts, largely through the suasion of educational leaders but increasingly through law, regulation, and judicial settlement. Yet who articulated this reigning consensus? What exactly has it stood for? Most important, why by 1980 had it come to seem so painfully out of touch with a public bristling at its expanding imperatives, arrogance, and apparent toleration of unsatisfactory schools?

In the summer of 1980 Chester E. Finn, Jr., sat down to address

10

these questions in a short article for *Change* magazine, a respected
education monthly. He was admirably suited to take on the task.
After receiving his doctorate at Harvard's Graduate School of Education, Finn had moved to the Brookings Institution. Then, in 1977,
at the age of thirty-three, Finn became New York Senator Daniel
Patrick Moynihan's senior legislative assistant in charge of, among
other things, the Senator's tuition–tax credit bill. While some Democratic colleagues on Capitol Hill—and more than a few Republicans—
considered Finn's educational prescriptions repugnant, they acknowledged that in matters of schooling he was one of Washington's most
original students of public policy. And unlike so many top-level educationists, they conceded, Finn was a master of the printed word and
a man of unlimited political energy. When "The Future of Education's
Liberal Consensus" appeared that fall, the article simultaneously gave
education's orthodoxy a new name and upset its establishment more
than any essay in many years.

First, Finn identified the origins of this "liberal consensus." In
terms of its major sources and prominent members, he said, it sprang
from the

> . . . Ford and Carnegie Foundations and four or five smaller ones;
> the elite graduate schools of education such as those at Stanford,
> Harvard, Chicago and Columbia; the major national organizations
> of teachers and educational institutions, such as the National Edu-
> cation Association, the American Association of School Adminis-
> trators, the National School Boards Association, and the American
> Council on Education; the various groups represented in the Lead-
> ership Conference on Civil Rights; the big labor unions; the political
> appointees in the education-related agencies of the federal executive
> branch (including, with a few exceptions, those of both Republican
> and Democratic presidents); half a dozen key Congressmen and
> perhaps two dozen Congressional staff members; a variety of "think
> tanks," notably including The Brookings Institution and the Aspen
> Institute; and the writers of education editorials for major metro-
> politan newspapers including The New York Times and The Wash-
> ington Post.

The liberal consensus had once stood, constructively, for equalizing educational opportunity and reducing the educational consequences

11

of individual differences through federal action and spending. The results, Finn explained, had been impressive. And yet something had gone awry: "The liberal consensus that has shaped national education policy for the past fifteen years . . . has begun to show signs of succumbing to a set of dubious ideas and undesirable practices." Finn then proceeded to dissect the wobbly theories and heavy-handed activities in which education's leading individuals and institutions had indulged.

In brief, the young education scholar located the waning strength of the liberal consensus in the education establishment's indifference or hostility toward scholastic success and educational excellence. In the rush to transform the principle of equal opportunity into a guarantee of equal results, he said, too many education experts had developed misguided priorities, championed flawed practices, and tried to overlook differing levels of student ability and achievement.

The liberal consensus, maturing in an era of social discord, cohered by avoiding fundamental issues of value. According to Finn and others, it remained insensible to early evidence that major initiatives such as compulsory busing, student rights, and the introduction of experimental, often nonacademic curricula had damaging effects. It allowed the growing teachers' unions to pretend that tenured instructors were, by definition, competent professionals and to negotiate legal contracts based on that fiction. Many true believers within the consensus claimed that insisting on clear, sometimes absolute, subject standards and then using tests to measure how well students had mastered them was discriminatory, for both practices made arbitrary judgments about the unique gifts, needs, and values of every individual. Besides, tests were culturally biased and psychologically damaging. All the while, the liberal consensus ignored, savaged, or derided critics who urged schools to reward academic talent and accomplishment—in short, those who argued for educational quality.

The liberal consensus feared giving offense to any particular group. Too mindful of the virtue of tolerance, it condoned outlandish points of view and accepted bizarre modes of behavior. It was especially accommodating to new, well-organized, hyperactive lobbies and special interest associations, skilled in the manipulation of elected and court officials and often centralized in the nation's capital. Groups as different as the Children's Defense Fund, the Council on Interracial Books for Children, the Harvard Center for Law and Education, the National Education Association, and the Mexican-American Legal Defense Fund shared the conviction that public schools must deal with new, redemptive, and usually nonscholastic issues.

Seeking entitlements, regulations, appropriations, jobs, curricular revisions, and more, such groups by the early seventies were able to bully their way into the center of the educational reform agenda, often assisted by sympathetic judges and legal displays by federal civil rights officials. School leaders permitted the ideal of ending involuntary segregation to give way to a principle of reverse discrimination in which specified individuals and groups were to be given special recognition and privileges. To the vocally aggrieved, the schools promised to be everyman's engine of social repair. Those who considered themselves victims—not only of racial prejudice but also of physical and economic condition, of language, of gender, of ethnic background, and even of conventional manners—began to look to the public schools for relief and reparation. In the interests of equity the liberal consensus supported their efforts promiscuously.

The taxpaying public did not. Its lukewarm sanction of the liberal program for public education developed from its residual faith in the power of schools to make all things better, from middle-class guilt over earlier lapses in social justice, from the protective distance between suburban and city school districts, from pre-OPEC economic prosperity—all of this. But broad-based support also flowed from the authoritative assurances of experts. *Trust us, we know what we're doing.*

To many, after a while, reform activities seemed disruptive or personally costly. A Youngstown, Ohio, steelworker, for example, might complain that his seventh-grade child had no homework, was routinely harassed in the school cafeteria, and was learning more in class about masturbation than about fractions. No one in power seemed to hear him. Ill-conceived federal initiatives, such as the attempted prohibition of father-and-son athletic banquets as sexually discriminatory, made some government activities appear ridiculous and meddlesome, not to say offensive.

Exactly when wide public endorsement of Great Society school reform ventures wilted, who can be sure? But clearly, by the time of the 1974 Boston busing riots frail goodwill toward the liberal consensus was foundering on the shoals of racial conflict, loss of parental control, involuntarism, indiscipline, and more. To sustain meliorist efforts in public schools, reformers increasingly resorted to fiscal threats and court orders. *We know what's best for you.* Alarmed that many educational leaders wanted to use schools as centers of social reconstruction, against electoral will and at the expense of academic integrity if necessary, citizens rebelled.

The liberal consensus lost its political base, and at the same time its theoretical cement began to crack. In the later seventies cumulative research pointed toward conclusions that reformers could not explain away: For fifteen years, despite massive spending and federal assistance, the performance record of the average U.S. school, especially at the secondary level, had declined. And not only were entrenched educational leaders unable to ascertain ways to reverse the slide; many of them seemed intent on protecting practices that contributed to it.

Like Nova Scotian or Breton tides, national moods about education shift powerfully from time to time, at first without notice. For several years now public ratification of vaunted school reforms has been ebbing. Taxpayers are weary of school equity crusades and other voluptuous plans for social renovation. According to a decade of Gallup Polls, parents consider lack of discipline the number one problem in schools. Almost 70 percent of them want more emphasis on academic basics (even though precisely what "basics" are remains a matter of fierce argument). Consequently, an impressive reconsideration of what schools should be is taking place at the grassroots level and beyond. In April 1981 *The New Republic,* an eminent journal that has helped to frame liberal social policy since the heyday of John Dewey, broke editorial traditions to devote a special issue to what it called "the unremitting bad news about public education." In 1983 a report of the National Commission on Excellence in Education warned of "a rising tide of mediocrity that threatens our very future as a nation and a people." The ardent unionist Albert Shanker, President of the American Federation of Teachers, declared in an interview: "Addressing the problem of quality and academic excellence, and not rolling over every time some crazy group makes some demand for the schools, must be the first priority for educational improvement."

In the upper reaches of government, the media, and the education establishment itself, a new group of reformers now believes that schools (1) can be effective, orderly, and spirited places for students of all grades, races, and classes; (2) can increase student academic power—and thereby self-respect—by stressing a basic curriculum; (3) can sustain adult authority so that the experience and wisdom of the old can act as a buffer to the ignorance of the young; and (4) can help the majority of youth learn that hard work and exemplary character are prerequisites of the good life. They declare these possibilities *in spite of* increasing competition for public funds, *in spite of* declining student enrollments, *in spite of* the persistence of racial conflict, and *in spite of* the Augean task of persuading thousands of government officials and school districts to institute better school practices.

From the minimum competency testing movement in state legislatures to renewed debate over educational vouchers, assaults on the old order, deserved and undeserved, are coming thick and fast. But so far no single event has had the impact of the Republican conquest of the White House and Senate in November 1980. To be sure, school quality never surfaced as an explicit campaign issue. Yet the sorry state of so many schools, especially in central cities and working-class neighborhoods, acted as trenchant testimony about unpopular domestic policies hatched a decade or more earlier. Ronald Reagan, the Republican candidate, repeatedly promised, if elected, to dissolve the newborn Department of Education. But his threat was simple political pageantry, since ED merely administered programs that Congress enacted. Whether or not ED existed meant little in terms of actual federal—or local—education policy. And whether or not ED existed meant little in terms of improving academic methods, standards, or outcomes: Its congressionally created job and assistance programs were educational more in name than in effect.

Significantly, the Reagan victory made possible a new direction for public policy in education, first by giving heart to people who had resisted in vain the excesses of the liberal consensus. For the first time in a generation a president voiced his doubts that the federal

15

government had any appropriate role in education. That view in itself broke markedly with the past, since the liberal consensus's agenda had been implemented mainly through vigorous federal activity.

Upon inauguration the Republicans wasted no time in serving notice that henceforth ED would not be a comfortable shelter for Great Society–style egalitarians and advocates of increased federal power. Twelve days after the inauguration the Department rescinded the 1980 bilingual education regulations, which it had promulgated just before the election. (The guidelines had so resembled a compulsory national curriculum and threatened local control of teaching methods that even the most loyal members of the educational establishment had been taken aback.) The Administration sought to slash major elementary and secondary school initiatives such as compensatory education by 25 percent or more. It proposed giving general aid to states and localities instead of grants to special programs and populations, reflecting its conviction that Washington should act more passively in educational decision-making and rely on the states to carry out the intent of federal education policies.

In 1981, with some reason, many educational leaders were aghast at what they saw as Republican fiscal hard-heartedness at the fate of students from low-income families, as in the case of school lunch cutbacks. As to educational philosophy, however, the Republican leadership at first showed little interest in rallying around the icons of educational fundamentalists who advocated the restoration of school prayer, the adoption of creationist textbooks, patriotic drills in the classroom, or the prohibition of collective bargaining by teachers.

Then, in 1982, the Reagan Administration gave much more evidence of trying to accommodate the educational right. By trying to bestow tax-exempt status on schools with openly discriminatory admissions policies, the White House played into the hands of those who maintained that the executive branch was being run by racists. To many sympathetic with the Administration's early education initiatives, the President's highly publicized endorsement of a school-prayer amendment was nothing short of embarrassing. By 1983, facing Washington's inconsistent education policies and philosophies, few who were part of the conservative reaction to liberal policy still had great

16

hope for inventive federal leadership in state-level and district-level improvements.

Inside and outside the new Administration one issue remained profoundly divisive: public assistance to private schools through tuition tax credits and other means. Dissenters from the liberal consensus fought among themselves (thus splitting what was possibly an emerging educational consensus built around quality). Some contended that the credits would contaminate one of the deepest wellsprings of national unity and validate the absolute demise of the common school. Public schools were a unique American triumph, they said, and governments at all levels had an interest in maintaining and improving them. The expansion of private education would result in fraud and hucksterism, added regulations and bureaucracies, and further social splintering. Adherents of pro–private school policies argued that nonpublic education gave new educational hope to the poor and was likely to increase public school quality, especially in the cities, through increased competition.

In some metropolitan areas middle-class families of all races were increasingly receptive to private alternatives, often turning to them with guilt but also with certainty that they were investing in their child's academic or behavioral welfare. Twenty-three percent of parents with school-age children claimed they would be likely to switch to private schools if tuition tax credits of $250 to $500 were enacted, a 1981 Gallup Poll showed. (This *interest* should not imply more *movement* than has occurred. Current estimates show that private school enrollments are still *slightly* below their mid-sixties peak of about 13 percent. The Christian schools—by far the fastest-growing component of the private sector—attract students in consequence of many different impulses, mostly nonacademic.)

What made the "private" issue so large was the way it reflected lost faith in the public system's ability to regulate itself. To much danger, popular sentiment in the early eighties was increasingly polarizing education into "good" private schools and "bad" public schools. Some school reformers were in fact giving up on old palliatives and calling for radical surgery. They contended that systemic rigidity— stale educational theories, restrictive union contracts, ironclad seniority rules, government mandates, due-process protections, and much more—made the reform of ineffective public schools impossible. To them, a share of the public system had lost touch irretrievably with the concept of quality.

Still, many public school educators resisted essential reforms. Some knew all too well how many parents expected schools to cure problems rooted in social miseries over which faculties had little or no control. Others, mischievously or ingenuously, professed that their own schools already provided "quality education." To more than a few, keeping a job meant preserving the status quo, no matter what the level of educational delivery. Those whose salaries and reputations had grown along with the liberal consensus had much to lose and little to gain from current calls for school improvement. Entrenched school personnel trusted the combined power of state and federal bureaucracies, special interest leaders, and court precedents to vanquish even their most intransigent critics.

Other professional educators—not allergic to the phrase "basic education"—were alert to new opportunities for reform. Research was proving that school decline could be—and in places had been—reversed. Suddenly they could point to certain schools and districts in which rehabilitation had already occurred. These reformers at once rejected the reductive nostalgia of many "back-to-basics" efforts and the pseudo-reform of the recent past. Few of them accepted the idea that the private sector, by necessity, must lead the way in school improvement. Their mood was optimistic rather than defeatist. For the time being they were on the offensive.

Much depended on their success, and not only the well-being of Carrick High School's students. In 1983, 38 million young citizens attended 86,000 elementary and secondary schools scattered across the continent. Some of them were improving their dexterity with crayons, others discovering that oxygen allows objects to burn and rust, and still others learning that *le chat* is not *le chien*. Some of them were turning off. At the moment, all of them were facing a national school system in which the gap between achievers and nonachievers was fearsome—and apparently widening.

School reform had become an urgent national imperative. Stable and productive citizenship, the pursuit of happiness and social virtue, and the ability of individuals to control their own destinies all depended in part on effective schools. The children in schools of the eighties would determine the durability of the democratic experiment in the twenty-first century. And too many schools were breeding superfluous, irrelevant citizens. Or, to put it more starkly, they were helping to produce what appeared to be the first genuine American *lumpenprole-tariat*. If large numbers of young people continued to leave school unequipped to participate in the labor force, if they grew to adulthood finding their society illegible or malevolent, then the outlook for the commonwealth was grim indeed.

TWO

The Progressive Century

I N THE CURRENT CRITIQUE of elementary and secondary education it is tempting to search for proximate causes in recent history. One well-worn theme explains school deterioration as an unintended outcome of utopian social doctrines and equity-based public policy adventures, suddenly given free rein during the sixties. Another explains decline in quality as yet another symptom of cultural disarray, confusion, and demoralization. While such propositions contain some truth, it is shortsighted to locate agents of school decline solely in contemporary events and attitudes.

During the last generation so much has changed: popular conceptions of liberty and equality, families, television, drugs, and more. But one matrix of today's educational woes lies well in the past, specifically in the corruption of John Dewey's educational precepts during the second quarter of the century and in the triumph of counterfeit "progressive" theories that have enticed educators to the present. The ongoing dispute between traditional and modern education was relatively well framed by the late thirties. Myriad educational practices and objectives thought to have been invented by a recent wave of romantic, humanizing reformers are older still.

The educational present began about ninety years ago as part of the general turn-of-the-century movement called Progressivism. At that time genteel reformers of social standing, political leverage, and mental acumen acted to advance honest government, public hygiene, and democratic virtue, not least through what they thought to be the school's wonder-working powers. Since then the protean term "progressive education" has been applied to diverse efforts to expand the public school's services, among them, improving the quality of community life by training, acculturating, and ministering to the children of the masses and using new discoveries in psychology and the social sciences to meet more specific needs of these children.

In redefining ideal school practices and aims, Dewey was the Progressives' most influential pathfinder. His formulation of Progressive principles derived from theories of individuality developed by enlightened eighteenth- and nineteenth-century philosophers. Before his death in 1952 Dewey and his works in educational theory had achieved sufficient stature to make Deweyism the conceptual axis around which all subsequent discussions of school techniques and goals were bound to revolve.

First as practitioner at his University of Chicago laboratory school, ultimately as the panoptic sage of Columbia University's Teachers College, Dewey advocated teaching methods that encouraged children to learn subjects in more interesting ways. As early as 1897, in *My Pedagogic Creed,* he declared that the most fertile soil for learning was the small child's own experience. By harnessing juvenile instincts to question, explore, and communicate, Dewey said, schools could stimulate student interest and, consequently, student effort. Increased effort, Dewey pointed out, would lead to improved educational outcomes for children of all capabilities. A less formal curriculum and a school climate more attentive to mental and temperamental differences among children, one which encouraged children to participate actively in the educational process, were measures that Dewey successfully promoted throughout his long career.

Why did Dewey's pedagogy receive such wide attention and finally become the core of modern school theory? First of all, Dewey was

21

the most significant intellect of his generation to concern himself with schools. Second, his recommendations were plastic enough to suit—and legitimize—the views of others, including many of his students, who came to think of themselves as Dewey's apostles. Third, and possibly most important, Dewey emphasized time and again the heroic mission of the teacher and school in social progress, thus inspiring and emboldening professional educators during the years when they were extending school services to children of all social classes, a democratic venture without historical precedent.

The popularity of progressive methods spread after World War I, especially in private schools patronized by college-educated parents and the literati. In a flood of articles, lectures, and colloquiums, the intellectual community worked vigorously for their adoption in all school districts. When the Progressive Education Association was founded in 1919, its first honorary president was Charles W. Eliot, former president of Harvard, a man of immense authority who a generation before had taken the lead in improving the quality of U.S. high schools by strengthening course content and academic requirements. During the twenties, in such cosmopolitan suburbs as Bronxville, Shaker Heights, Winnetka, and Pasadena, the "new education" gained a foothold at the primary level. By 1938 it had gained sufficient cachet and respectability to permit *Time* magazine, not a trend-setting journal, to write an approving cover article on progressive school practices.

But long before that, as school reforms espoused by Dewey were becoming conventional, the theories behind them were being trivialized and adulterated. Dewey was not his own evangelist. The chief interlocutor between the master's opaque writings and the teaching profession at large was another Teachers College professor, William Heard Kilpatrick. A dazzling lecturer, Kilpatrick conducted legendary classes through the twenties and thirties that, finally, overflowed Teachers College's own Horace Mann auditorium and were assigned to Columbia's largest amphitheater. As the best-known exponent of Deweyism in the nation's most prestigious education school, Kilpatrick had an enormous influence on a generation of graduate students, many of them destined to lead other teachers colleges and the education establishment before mid-century.

Kilpatrick propounded a simplified version of progressive education that even students at provincial normal schools could grasp. The outlook was Manichaean: In one dark universe, ten-year-olds sat at attention in straight-backed chairs, memorizing facts from drab primers, speaking only when spoken to. Solemn schoolmasters drilled students without mercy, impelling effort, if need be, with hickory sticks and dunce caps. In the universe of light, schools served the "felt needs" of students, possibly through Kilpatrick's own "project method" developed in 1918. This novel pedagogy rejected the concept of studying subjects in organized capsules, such as reading, spelling, and arithmetic. In its most advanced form, touched with the glamour of bohemianism and of the infant field of psychology, it allowed children to decide what topics should be studied in school, in other words, to determine their own curriculum and activities.

The project method went like this: A teacher might bring a Navajo blanket to school. Interested by the object, the class would decide to study Indians. To set their own learning goals and divide the subject into manageable areas, students would form committees. Then they might visit museums or go to libraries to discover how Indians ate, dressed, and lived. Later, each committee might report its discoveries to the class, build a teepee, or produce a play about Indians. "Learning by doing," went the slogan. Factual information and cognitive skills were supposed to filter into young minds through experiential osmosis.

In Kilpatrick's wonderful world, the modern learning process was free of tension. It was painless. It was liberating. How appealing! How magical! And how specious! For pure cornfed "progressive" insensibility—looking straight at intellect and seeing in it something repressive and irrelevant—Kilpatrick's positions deserve review. "The doctrine of mental discipline" and the study of academic subjects inhibited creativity, he said. Books were the "enemies of living inquiry." Because of their lack of practical value, classical languages, ancient history, algebra and geometry, even physics should be excised from the general secondary school curriculum. With pious self-righteousness, Kilpatrick and other child-centered Deweyans undertook a crusade against traditional methods *and* subjects. For this they cannot be excused. Before 1930 they had dispatched progressive education on its positively anti-intellectual track.

Kilpatrick's burning interest in individual initiative appeared to extend Dewey's work, and in some ways it did. But as Lawrence Cremin points out in his magisterial history, *The Transformation of the School,* the two men's pedagogy varied at a critical point. Dewey said learning should begin in the child's personal experience and proceed toward the traditional bodies of knowledge, such as literature, history, or biology, that represent the cumulative experience of the culture. According to Kilpatrick, the child should proceed pretty much as he wished. Dewey had charted a road from self to subject matter. Those who, like Kilpatrick, claimed that the school should simply facilitate the natural unfolding of the child's instincts were arriving at a dead-end defense of narcissism, in which all standards are self-originated and self-satisfied.

Then, in 1932, another Teachers College luminary, George S. Counts, complicated matters. "To an extent characteristic of no other institution, save that of the state itself, the school has the power to modify the social order," Dewey had once said. Schools should cultivate in youth willingness to sacrifice for the public good and prepare them for membership in the democratic fraternity, he thought. But how exactly should schools proceed? Counts gave one answer in a seminal lecture to the 1932 convention of the Progressive Education Association, published later in expanded form as *Dare the School Build a New Social Order?*

Specifically, Counts argued that, as they train young people, schools *inevitably* "shape attitudes, develop tastes and even impose ideas." Correct. But Counts went on. Since student indoctrination was unavoidable, why not use schools to advance more responsible political and economic ideas, in fact, lead the way in social reformation? Adults in schools, said Counts, could battle actively against class and privilege, teach cooperation instead of competition, wean youth from obsolete moral and religious precepts, instruct them in the evils of private enterprise, and consequently prepare students for the advent of democratic socialism.*

All through the thirties the idea of social reconstructionism was

---

* Dewey never warmed to Counts's vision. In a society with so many competing political and educative agencies, he concluded, it was not practical. Regrettably, Dewey did not seem shaken by what one later critic termed "brainwashing, democratic-style."

the central article of educationist chat. After the onset of the Depression it superseded, or rather came to sit side by side with, child-centered privatism in the theoretical schemes of advanced Progressive analysts. The pursuit of individual realization that the Progressives had so extolled in the twenties gave way to new interest in collective social action. The Teachers College Progressives founded a bimonthly discussion group and in 1934 began publishing a polemical journal sympathetic to New Deal–style social and economic reform.

At mid-century a younger Progressive named Theodore Brameld rose to prominence as the chief proponent of reconstructionism. Brameld frankly endorsed "inducing and controlling changes in human relations and in the structure of social institutions." Though his writing was so cryptic that some skeptical readers might wonder if Brameld was keeping controversial programmatic goals to himself, the major reconstructionist themes emerge: faith in a labor or workers' movement to promote democratic equality; extreme interest in national planning, including federal control of education; desire for international or planetary consensus; antagonism to traditional authorities, especially religion; and belief in educational programs that emphasize change and prepare students for the "new order," left undefined. To their credit, the reconstructionists were in the advance guard calling attention to the injustices and inequalities that Negro citizens suffered. Their one-world propositions never captured the fancy of classroom teachers at large. Nonetheless, they gave Progressivism an undeserved reputation for anti-American radicalism.

By the fifties countless cartoons and books like Patrick Dennis's *Auntie Mame* made fun of progressive schools where children took off their clothes and played "fish families" all day. But darkly, a few mid-century school critics, galvanized by anti-Communist sentiment, imagined something more sinister: fellow-traveling progressive teachers recruiting students in behalf of internationalism, reading pro-Soviet literature to eighth-graders, softly and persuasively, with fanatical glints in their eyes.

The impact of the Deweyan theorists on schools and buildings should not be overdramatized. Progressivism tended to moderate itself at the local level, as theories were bent to adapt to neighborhood realities. The rise of the social sciences, especially psychology, drew attention to the instrumental possibilities of schools; interest in humanizing industrial civilization resulted in school-based meals and health services; an emerging corporate economy generated much enthusiasm for vocational education and the organized development of practical trade skills; destitute localities during the thirties first looked to Washington to provide needed aid for education; and U.S. involvement in global war after Pearl Harbor influenced intellectuals who wanted schools to nurture world fellowship and peace. But at the secondary level, the authority of the traditional academic program ensured its prestige in school life.

Very gradually, between 1915 and 1950, this changed. More revolutionary than any Deweyan debate over methods or aims was the structural transformation of the high school, as secondary schooling became mandatory and universal. By 1918 every state had enacted compulsory school laws requiring all children to attend school until well into adolescence. During the first twenty years of the century the average legal age for leaving school jumped from fourteen years and five months to sixteen years and three months. Between 1900 and 1930 the American high school population rose from 630,000 to almost 5 million, and it continued to expand.

For most leaders of the compulsory education movement, longer schooling was part of a humanitarian impulse to shelter and protect immigrant, mill-working, and farm-dwelling youths. Others advocating universal secondary schooling emphasized the more specialized labor needs of industrial employers and the collapse of the apprentice system of job training. Police agencies pressured educators and legislators to remove urchins from the streets. Trade unions lobbied to reduce job competition. To what effect? As the education historian Lawrence A. Cremin has said, "The dreams of democratic idealists may have resided in compulsory-education laws, but so did the makings of the blackboard jungle."

The problem was this. The newcomers at central high schools tended to be unable, reluctant, or hostile students. Typically they dropped out of school as quickly as they could. Why were the schools not meeting *their* needs? And what could schools do to address those needs? Was the traditional academic program—or even the vocational alternatives—appropriate for all children? And what new innovations might be devised to extend the schools' holding power and retention rates so that students would remain in school until graduation?*

By the end of World War II such questions haunted the nation's most powerful architects of education. In 1945 one of them, the vocational education leader Charles Prosser, enunciated a startling proposition: Because of limited ability or interest, a full 60 percent of U.S. teenagers could not benefit from existing academic or vocational programs in schools. How Prosser arrived at this amazing conclusion is anybody's guess, but his revelation reflected a then popular view of the average student's weak mind. Many educators of Prosser's generation, convinced by the authority of newly introduced intelligence tests, had concluded that a huge number of students could not master the normal academic curriculum. Some, like Prosser, bristled at the use of vocational programs as dumping grounds for educational misfits and potential dropouts.

Their solution came with the postwar "life adjustment" craze, which sought to install nonacademic programs in high school curricula for the less than gifted. In effect, life adjustment tried to carry Kilpatrick's old crusade against liberal studies to the secondary level. Courses once introduced for slow learners were now to be standard high school fare. Life-adjustment advocates said that what high schools needed was an entirely new "general" course of study. It should be based on "functional experiences in the areas of the practical arts, home and family life, health and physical fitness, and civic competence," according to the U.S. Office of Education's 1947 declaration,

---

* True, these were not new questions or new concerns. The postwar debate was the culmination of a trend of thirty years, during which the Progressives had tilted decidedly toward the view that the high school's time-honored emphasis on academic mastery and the liberal arts curriculum was too narrow. As early as 1918 the National Education Association's Committee on the Reorganization of Secondary Education had issued its seminal *Cardinal Principles of Secondary Education*, which listed seven separate objectives in the education of adolescents. Six of them were to promote what might today be called physical, consumer, career, civic, affective, and moral education. The seventh could be called minimum competency. Thus, by the forties the nonacademic ("extra") curriculum had great appeal to many professional educators. The academic function of the high school, however modest, competed with six apparent coequals.

Life Adjustment Education for Every Youth. Contrary to time-honored educational concepts, no broad mental qualities needed to be developed, the historian Richard Hofstadter protested. There were only specific things to be known, say, sewing, fixing a flat tire, or calculating the cost of a cut of meat. And instead of leaving certain spheres of education to the family and other community agencies, Hofstadter said, life adjustment hoped to convert the home and student social life into objects of elaborate study.

Through the early fifties, in innumerable conferences, teacher workshops, pilot programs, and hortatory bulletins, the U.S. Office of Education tried to colonize state education agencies and local school districts with this latest version of progressive education. Steered by the friendly hand of the federal government and supported by powerful national lobbies such as the American Association of Colleges for Teacher Education and the National School Boards Association, life adjustment briefly flourished in putative curriculum reform throughout the land. Radio repair was substituted for physics, and business English for Milton. Course topics such as "clicking with the crowd" and "personal grooming" joined—and occasionally replaced—composition and geometric proofs in modish high schools.

In its impatience with the liberal arts, its supposition that academic courses could not interest students of modest intellect, and its encroachment on other educative spheres to minister to the "whole child," life adjustment embodied progressive education's worst qualities. The intellectual community that had vigorously supported school reform a generation earlier, feeling duped, turned against Progressivism with a vengeance. Subsequently defenders of the tainted Deweyan faith fought dissent from the strategic fortresses they had secured in the second quarter of the century: the schools of education and offices of government.

As early as 1927 the Ohio State education professor Boyd H. Bode, perhaps the wisest of the first-generation Deweyans, warned against the Rousseauan sentiment that imagined "sage and saint in the nature of the child, needing only to shed its wrappings to be clearly perceived." Eleven years later, in his brilliant book-length essay *Progressive Educa-*

28

tion at the Crossroads, Bode briskly rejected child-centered learning altogether: "It would hardly be an exaggeration to say that the purpose of sound education is precisely to emancipate the pupil from dependence on immediate interest," he said. In 1938, too, Dewey himself made his most agitated statements against Progressive inversions, criticizing schools that "tend to make little or nothing of organized-subject matter of study; to proceed as if any form of direction or guidance by adults were an invasion of individual freedom."

The same year conflicts between factions of the Teachers College confraternity burst into public view. The education professor William C. Bagley joined with other nationally known humanists to found the so-called Essentialist Committee, later formalized as the Society for the Advancement of American Education. To Bagley, how best to mate Dewey's relativism with academic excellence was a central question that modern educators needed to answer but had, so far, avoided. Bagley did not look back fondly on "traditional" nineteenth-century schools. He loathed the routinized catechism that passed for a course of study in old-fashioned schools as much as he hated pigeon-holing students in different curricula on account of IQ tests. But as he saw it, current educational theories were degrading the liberal studies and producing a weak-minded civilization.

All schools, said Bagley, should "prepare boys and girls for adult responsibilities through systematic training in such subjects as reading, writing, arithmetic, history and English, requiring mastery of subjects, and when necessary, stressing discipline and obedience, with informal learning recognized but regarded as supplementary rather than central." These "essentials," he argued, were most likely to produce the literate and orderly electorate that any democratic polity required. This view was too narrow or too severe for Dewey to accept. Although the Essentialists carefully absolved Dewey of his disciples' excesses, the master dismissed Bagley's counterview as "reactionary." Thereafter Progressives and Essentialists considered themselves members of distinct, warring camps.

Had departments of pedagogy and state education agencies pushed life adjustment curricula with less fervor, Essentialism might have remained out of favor. But the life-adjustment totem ran against the grain of middle-class aspirations for the school. From the day the postwar baby boom set off for its first day in kindergarten, new millions of voter-parent-taxpayers became intense school observers. Many of them considered the school the vehicle whereby they themselves had achieved levels of affluence their own parents could not have dreamed of. When these parents discovered that progressive educators often disparaged their conviction that schools should be repositories of the academic skills they felt their children needed to get ahead, they shifted loyalties. Along with intellectuals, they shunned the educational novelties of their day. To both groups the term "progressive education" abruptly lost its old connection of fresh, enlightened pedagogy. Instead, it turned into a slur for sloppy schooling in general.

In 1949 several books, including Mortimer Smith's *And Madly Teach,* sounded the first alarums. Said Smith, mass education at the secondary level had forced educators to face incommodious realities. The choice had been either to teach basic subjects to those whose home lives and cultural backgrounds were not likely to hold the liberal studies and intellectual attainments in high esteem or else to design a different curriculum, a "useful" and "functional" course of study more immediate to the daily experience of the working and lower classes. Progressive educators, he concluded, had chosen the second, easier route. Extracting from Dewey's corpus the idea that effective education begins with the "immediate interests" of the child, they had relinquished the ideal of academic power for all students.

Of the mid-century Essentialists Arthur Bestor was the most eminent. A professor at Teachers College, then a historian at the University of Illinois, Bestor published *Educational Wastelands* (1953) to national acclaim, following it with the more comprehensive *The Restoration of Learning* two years later. Bestor said it was simple to explain the rise of life adjustment education in spite of the more prosaic subject tastes of parents. Communities had lost control of their schools. The educational enterprise had moved from the hands of laymen and scholars into what Bestor called an "interlocking directorate" of education professors, officials, and administrators: They had accumulated sufficient power through state-enforced certification requirements to disseminate an official view for teachers and to exclude anyone unwilling to submit to it.

Supported by state education bureaucracies and by superintendents and principals who understood that the party line was essential
to swift career advancement, Bestor said, education professors did
not "hesitate to defy the intellectual conscience of the university and
of the nation." They had turned the speculative nature of educational
philosophy into dogma. They had pursued research projects that "had
so little to do with advancing knowledge and were so naive in technique
that they rapidly became the laughing-stock of university campuses."
Under the guise of being sensitive to student psychology, concluded
Bestor, a repellently antidemocratic educational system was under construction.

This was a lacerating indictment of those who held power and
made policy in U.S. education. Needless to say, it touched an exposed
nerve. No leader of any Progressive viewpoint—Dewey, Bode, and
Kilpatrick were all dead by now—had Bestor's incandescent way with
words. Despite much huffing and puffing in the education establishment, its apologists could produce no convincing refutation of his
charges.

The Essentialists now smelled blood on the trail. In July 1956
a handful of them, including Smith and Bestor, met in Washington
to create a Council for Basic Education. The charter membership
was a roll call of the nation's scholarly praetorian guard: Crane Brin-
ton, Malcolm Cowley, Howard Mumford Jones, Alfred A. Knopf,
Joseph Wood Krutch, Peter Viereck, and many more. In the late
fifties the body became a successful forum for intellectuals to wage
battle against the "interlocking directorate" and try to reform teacher
education. But the CBE was assisted by a separate international event.
The Russians, in October 1957, launched Sputnik I, the first space
satellite. To alarmed editorialists, government officials, and business
leaders, the Soviet Union's rapid scientific advance in the postwar
years seemed inextricably linked to its more rigorous educational system.

For some time, the respected Vice Admiral Hyman G. Rickover,
a leader of the Navy's nuclear-power program, had argued exactly
this point. In 1959 his best-selling book *Education and Freedom* limned
a grim cold war picture: The United States had ignored its "first
line of defense" for the quality of education and in doing so was in

profound danger of losing the battle for military supremacy with the Soviet Union. Rickover agreed with the Essentialists that schools needed to reemphasize academic power. But the direction of his argument was more technocratic, less humanistic. The Essentialists wanted a common curriculum of the humanities and sciences. Rickover and his champions in the federal government—he had remarkable power in key congressional committees—were more interested in creating an able corps of scientific specialists and engineers to safeguard national defense.

In such a climate the Carnegie Corporation asked the former Harvard president James B. Conant—as august a figure in education as his predecessor Charles W. Eliot—to undertake a two-year study of the high school and to make recommendations for its future. The choice of the man was significant: Conant had long been active in the National Education Association's blue-ribbon Educational Policies Commission and, like few academic mandarins, straddled the intellectual community and the education establishment without effort. The 1959 Conant Report became the most authoritative design for secondary education in the postwar era. It provided a basic blueprint for modern high schools still in use today.

What Conant recommended was an academically centered institution *for all students,* including both a minimum four-year course of study in English and social studies and a one-year course in mathematics and science. In addition, he urged schools to require at least six academic periods daily, adopt ability grouping devices, and improve conditions for academically talented students. Simultaneously, as Cremin points out, Conant remained faithful to authentic Progressive ideals, stressing the need for improved counseling systems, individualized student programs, increased course diversity, and special considerations for slow learners. In endorsing the "comprehensive" public high school as a learning center for adolescents of all capabilities, Conant rejected both private schooling for an academic elite and the European system of categorizing students into academic, technical, and terminal groups, then schooling them accordingly. Conant's call for universal government-operated high school programs and for Progressive methods *with academic ends* reflected new public concern with learning outcomes.

Then, in the early sixties, two landmark educational histories appeared. Each of them treated Progressivism as a phenomenon that had altered the very essence of U.S. education and as a movement in crisis. In 1961 Lawrence Cremin completed *The Transformation of the School,* the first—and still the best—critical narrative of the new education. Cremin insisted that twentieth-century school reforms added up to a great liberating force in democratic culture. But, he acknowledged, the movement had lost its direction and clear-sightedness. In his final, impassioned paragraph, Cremin admitted that the theory and practices that Progressivism propounded needed "drastic reappraisal."

The next year the Columbia historian Richard Hofstadter produced a less sanguine evaluation. *Anti-Intellectualism in American Life* won the 1964 Pulitzer Prize for nonfiction. The book's final section contained a mordant exegesis of "the road to life adjustment," which Hofstadter placed within the context of long-standing American animus toward mental refinement and intellect. Hofstadter warned that life adjustment had gone underground but remained vital in the attitudes of educators and the public. And make no mistake about it, said Hofstadter, life adjustment was a mortal threat to individual and collective welfare. "The new education," he asserted,

> is indeed trying to educate "the whole child," in that it is trying to shape the character and personality of its charges; and that what it aims to do is not primarily to fit them into a disciplined part of the world of production and competition, ambition and vocation, creativity, and analytical thought, but rather to help them learn the ways of the world of consumption and hobbies, of enjoyment and social complaisance—in short, to adapt gracefully to the passive and hedonistic style summed up by the significant term *adjustment.* [Hofstadter's italics]

So it seemed at the start of the sixties that the substance of American education was on the verge of long-overdue refurbishment. In the year Hofstadter wrote, almost fifty years had elapsed since the appearance of the "project method" and the NEA's *Cardinal Principles.* His words seemed to herald an era of renewed academic rigor and the restoration of classical educational values. The supreme irony

33

of that hopeful moment was this, however: In the next few years, what followed was the start of the greatest tidal wave of anti-intellectualism that the country has ever experienced. A generation later, in the eighties, some education analysts, putting the airbrush to history, would hold up the fifties and early sixties as a golden age of academic achievement, social stability, and educational quality.

THREE

The Era of Equality and Ecstasy

THE DRASTIC REAPPRAISAL of Progressivism did come, in fact, was under way even as Cremin and Hofstadter were writing. And its fresh reform impulse came about, of course, through efforts to eradicate differences in educational attainment on account of birth or background. In 1954 the juggernaut of educational equity lumbered into public view with *Brown* v. *Board of Education of Topeka*. In its unanimous decision the Supreme Court had ruled that "separate educational facilities are inherently unequal." This constitutional ban on racially segregated schools was then followed by a court order requiring states to begin school integration "with all deliberate speed."

Immediately states with school segregation laws on the books resisted. Georgia made it a felony for any school official to spend tax money for public schools in which races were mixed. North Carolina withheld state funds from any school district that integrated its schools. Virginia closed its public schools completely and subsequently enrolled white children in segregated state-funded "private" academies. The 1957 Little Rock crisis, graphically recorded in news photographs of bayonet-carrying paratroopers escorting nine courageous black teenagers into Central High School through howling white mobs, shamed millions of Americans. It convinced some that, if anything, school desegregation should proceed at a faster pace.

The odium of raw racism galvanized broad political and public endorsement, at least outside the Southeastern states, of increased federal activity in schools. Equal educational opportunity for blacks appealed to sentiments of fair play: According to the national folklore, the school properly assisted social mobility for all deserving, hard-working youngsters, including those coming from the most modest or deprived circumstances. Swiftly, editorial writers, religious leaders, university professors, government authorities, and, finally, middle-of-the-road voters turned the goal of racial equality in schools—and else-where—into a litmus test of moral citizenship. By the enactment of the Civil Rights Act of 1964—specifying that no person should be discriminated against on the basis of race, color, or national origin in any program that receives federal assistance, meaning that all federal aid might be withheld from districts or states failing to integrate their schools—desegregation had become a guiding star of social justice.

Thirty years after Counts's *Dare the School Build a New Social Order?,* the old dream of using schools as the driving wedge of social reconstruction seemed to be coming to life. No educational leader, it is safe to say, remained wholly immune to the glowing hope that an unprecedented era of racial harmony might result from school alterations. In this inflamed and optimistic moment, new ground rules about school reform began to harden. To summarize: (1) White and nonwhite students should not attend separate schools. (2) The best remedy for black deficits in social and educational achievement was to separate black children from the "pathological condition"* of black culture and assimilate them into "healthy" white culture. (3) The federal government, especially the federal courts, should participate actively through their Fourteenth Amendment responsibilities to ad-vance individual equity interests and redistribute educational resources more fairly. (4) Supposedly impartial and value-free social science findings (which influenced the policy debate on integration and equity

* These were Gunnar Myrdal's words in *An American Dilemma* (1944). Such sentiment had become commonplace in the social scientific community, at least until the black separatist movements of the sixties.

from *Brown* on) should be considered the most reliable pointer for educational policy-makers. Therefore, educationists should pay attention to new research, even when risking conflict with the wishes of local school clienteles.

The mood among the social engineers who attempted school reorganization was scientific, experimental, and utopian all at the same time. The outcome of their efforts, it was thought, could be the reduction or elimination of welfare rolls, poverty, and crime. Perhaps the best example of the new Progressivism's vigor, popularity, and style was the landmark Elementary and Secondary Education Act of 1965.

The coming of ESEA marked a significant turn in federal education activity. After 1965 judicial and legislative efforts to promote color-blind educational opportunities in schools were not enough. Education was now in a process of conversion to take on more ambitious ventures in social amelioration. Increasingly, schools (and new federal policy adventures) were seen as vehicles of more equal social attainments and rewards. Federal activism reflected Washington's intense and even touching faith during the mid-sixties in education's wonder-working powers, as did other education-centered War on Poverty programs like Head Start and the Job Corps. "The answer for all our national problems comes down to a single word," proclaimed a schoolmaster turned President, Lyndon B. Johnson. "That word is education."

ESEA was most of all a politically acceptable way to release federal funds to local schools. Its main stated purpose, however, was to "compensate" low-income youths for possible deprivation resulting from their social environments, entitling them to special programs designed to reduce their handicaps. Of ESEA's five original sections, the first was the most important. Title I* deployed massive federal funds for remedial programs in schools with a large number of poor students. Title I thus became the prototypical "categorical" education program, aimed at specially targeted populations. ESEA's lesser titles made funds available for textbook acquisition and library expansion; between 1965 and 1967 about 3,600 new public libraries were created through federal largesse. The act funded new educational services such

---

* Renamed "Chapter I" in 1981.

as dropout centers. It paid for a giant network of educational research laboratories. It provided modest monies to upgrade state education agencies.

Even Essentialists approved of ESEA. The Council for Basic Education, for example, endorsed the venture despite Executive Director Mortimer Smith's prescient reservations. Title I funds might be misspent, he said. The act made no effort to improve the quality of teacher education. And the premise that poor and black children had "special" educational needs was doubtful. But in 1965 few educational leaders still paid much attention to the Essentialists or, for that matter, considered them a threat. Intent on exorcising life-adjustment attitudes from the schools, basic educators were paying too little attention to new equity concerns and the changes they might render in school operations. While Essentialism almost certainly continued to reflect the prevalent views of middle-class parents, its constituency was not vocal. A confident and newly aggressive "liberal consensus" elbowed Essentialism to the edge of the educational conversation, where it remained until the mid-seventies. For a decade or more, subject-centered educators talked mainly to themselves, defensively and petulantly. Even to many earlier allies they sounded cranky and out of touch with the *Zeitgeist.*

Political perceptions compounded their problems. Essentialists had long been unsympathetic to all pressures that could undercut the central academic purpose of the school. But at the peak of enthusiasm for the Great Society, propelled by courageous black leaders and a radiant belief in social change, any group that resisted making the schoolyard a locus of social redemption was in danger of appearing misanthropic or racist.

Indeed, the crankiest—and loudest—opposition to new equity impulses was coming from white, Protestant, rural cohorts, many of whom entertained arcadian dreams of education's reversion to the Little Red Schoolhouse. Some simplifiers claimed that progressive education was consciously fostering national illiteracy, challenging the autonomy of the family, and indoctrinating the young in the cause of secularism and collectivism. Race-haters rallied alongside the nostalgics. To the bright-eyed reformers of the sixties, who tended to see the world in outlines just as simple as did their conservative enemies, subject-centered education best fitted within the slot reserved for moral, political, and racial purifiers on the right-wing fringe.

The season of extremism was opening.

From the right came Max Rafferty, elected California State Superintendent of Public Instruction in 1962, who wrote a syndicated column for more than fifty newspapers from coast to coast. A screaming-eagle reactionary, Rafferty idealized a never-never land of schooling where teachers, to cite one of his many columns, "followed the first Conestoga wagons westward, long rifle and McGuffey reader at the ready, fighting big, rawboned boys bare-knuckled for the right to teach them Latin conjugations, trading grammar for grain, Chaucer for chickens, arithmetic for apple cider." In Rafferty's columns, reasoned discussions of Essentialism or the Conant Report, the *Brown* case or ESEA, the Bill of Rights or due process simply never surfaced. Any skeptical reader searching for an authentic reform program somewhere in his essays ultimately discovered that Rafferty, quite earnestly, was trying to wish back the Conestoga wagon. Nonetheless, in a decade of turmoil his columns jolted millions of like-minded readers with their inflammatory style and left them with comforting images of a mythologized American past.

From others came a more devastating attack. Romantic and New Left radicals resembled Rafferty in choosing not to address the inevitable compromises and constraints of real-world meliorism. But by contrast, they leveled an astonishing set of charges at U.S. schools that, if true, would have rendered seventy years of hard-won Progressive accomplishments meaningless or invalid. In their critique, three generations of humanizing efforts and school improvements—playgrounds, kindergartens, infirmaries, cafeterias, student clubs, athletic programs, counseling services, varied and stimulating elective curricula, vastly expanded educational opportunities for working-class and lower-class children, and more—counted for nothing. To radical libertarians, the U.S. school remained an authoritarian, life-denying institution.

The first of many calls to "deschool" society came from Paul Goodman, a proclaimed anarchist and influential New York intellectual who wrote *Growing Up Absurd* (1960) and then *Compulsory Mis-*

39

education (1964). As Goodman saw it, progressive education had been an incomplete revolution. It had placed *some* premium on individual wants and needs, but in rhetoric more than in practice. Now, said Goodman, society owed young people the right to gravitate to whatever suited them. And it should begin by rejecting the "mass superstition, that the way to educate the majority of the young is to pen them up in schools during their adolescence and early adulthood." The abandonment of compulsory education, Goodman concluded, would counteract the feeling of powerlessness that most young people—and, for that matter, adults—had come to believe was an inevitable life sentence in consumer culture.

John Holt's best-selling *How Children Fail* (1964) went further. It presented the school as an intentionally coercive institution, one where adult influence on children was positively demonic. His declaration was unequivocal: "Children are subject peoples. School for them is a kind of jail." Adults were to blame:

> We adults destroy most of the intellectual and creative capacity of children by the things we do to them or make them do. . . .
> We encourage children to act stupidly, not only by scaring and confusing them, but by boring them, by filling their days with dull, repetitive tasks that make little or no claim on their attention or demands on their intelligence. Our hearts leap for joy at the sight of a roomful of children all slogging away at some imposed task.

This genre of writing, one with great emotional appeal, produced other rending narratives of helpless children regimented, harassed, and drained of self-esteem in broken-down buildings ruled by tyrannical bureaucrats. At best these treatments captured the despondent climate of city schools trying—and failing—to school the poor and nonwhite. James Herndon's *The Way It Spozed to Be* (1968) was a poignant memoir of the author's years teaching in a dilapidated inner-city school. Jonathan Kozol's *Death at an Early Age* (1967), subtitled *The Destruction of the Hearts and Minds of Negro Children in the Boston Public Schools,* won a National Book Award. Suddenly anti-school literature was drawing a huge, sympathetic, and influential audience.

In cinematic form, Frederick Wiseman's *High School* (1968) extended the school's image as prison to a white, middle-class campus. Its climax was especially shocking, given liberal revulsion toward the Vietnam War in the late sixties. The school principal rose to read a letter from a young alumnus, a soldier stationed on an aircraft carrier in the China Sea. The graduate thanked the faculty for its guidance. He expressed his sense of honor in serving—even dying for—one's country. Should he die in battle the next day, the letter droned on, the young man would bequeath a scholarship fund to the school. "When you get a letter like this, it means we are very successful," said the principal. The soldier had learned the school's tacitly prescribed code of conduct, Wiseman was implying. And that, the viewer had learned through a stream of earlier none-too-subtle *cinéma vérité* images, was a mixture of the captive's total resignation and of the soldier's sheeplike deference to orders from above.

No single critique of the schools during the sixties, however, had the force of A. S. Neill's *Summerhill*. This book was a narrative of the principles and practices of an English free school, which had operated since 1924 along strict child-centered lines. It carried no original theory of education. If anything, it had the musty smell of forty-year-old Rousseauan-*cum*-Freudian tracts. When *Summerhill* was announced by its American publisher in 1960, not a single bookseller ordered an advance copy. *The New York Times* did not bother to review it until 1966. But by the end of the decade Neill's book had become required reading in at least 600 university courses. It had been translated into ten languages, including Japanese and Hebrew. It was selling at the rate of 200,000 copies per year.

What suddenly made *Summerhill* a book that no educator could ignore and a text of sacred instructions to its countercultural enthusiasts? First, Neill restated in readable and self-righteous prose the old case that baby-knows-best. Neill's "radical approach to child rearing," which professed that *all* childhood activity should be voluntary, fitted cozily with current cries for absolute freedom from swelling numbers of rebellious youth. Summerhill, too, seemed to provide an institutional model that could act as an alternative to established school systems. And finally, to his followers, Neill himself was a tweedy old guru of love, a teacher and wise man who had never compromised his ideals to accommodate "the system." Neill's gospel had magnetic attraction for those educational romantics—educators and students—unfamiliar with time-worn Progressive nostrums: that human beings should be open in their relationships, that teachers should care about the individual needs of their students, that young people only need to be left alone to connect with their unique creativity.

In the Summerhill spirit, George Leonard, a leading exponent of the "human potential" movement, wrote *Education and Ecstasy* (1968). The hip *Look* magazine editor decided to bring Neill up to date. His description of how the ideal grammar school might appear in the year 2001 deserves lengthy quotation, for it reflects the amazing designs that utopian visionaries were then concocting for the school of the future.

> We walk up a ramp to an entrance. Two postgrads, an eleven-year-old boy and girl, welcome us with hugs and kisses. The girl finds our electronic identification devices on a large board, and we clip them to our clothing. The boy gives each of us a flower—a large orchid-like bloom, orange speckled with deep red, for my wife; a lavender rose for me—the products, we know, of botanical experiments by a group of six- to ten-year-olds. We thank our hosts with another embrace and stroll through a grove of oaks toward the Basics Dome. . . .
>
> On the way, we pass children of various ages in various states of consciousness. Some are walking aimlessly, alone or in small groups, perhaps toward some destination, perhaps not. Others are running. We notice a group of around seven of the older children with two of the educators in impassioned encounter near one of the biggest trees. Almost in our pathway sits a little girl with long black hair and dark skin—probably of Mexican-Indian extraction. Her enormous black eyes seem to hold a powerful dream, and we tiptoe around her, so as not to disturb her inner voyaging. But she looks up and, for a moment, shares with us something mysterious. . . .
>
> Children can come when and if they please; there's no problem at all if parents wish to take their children on extended trips or simply keep them home for something that's going on there.
>
> While the children are on the school grounds, they are *absolutely* free to go and do *anything* they wish that does not hurt someone else. They are *free learners.* [Leonard's italics]

While Leonard was hallucinating, something less ecstatic was happening in the real world. In city and suburban high schools, race riots, antiwar demonstrations, and student walkouts had become commonplace. Seasoned educators who had once considered themselves unflappable were horrified by disorder patently beyond their control. In a California junior high school a teacher cuddled a thirteen-year-old child, reeking of patchouli oil, whom she found crawling down a corridor freaked out on LSD. An able Providence, Rhode Island, instructor faced his seventh-grade class. Suddenly, a black girl scrambled to the top of her desk, turned on her transistor radio full blast, and started to dance. When the teacher put his arm on her shoulder to restrain her, the student screamed: "Get your fucking hands off me, white boy." The teacher finished the class, marched into the principal's office, and quit.

External stresses gave rise to new and extreme education policies. The civil rights movement had tapped an aquifer of equity pressures. Vietnam had led many in the intellectual community to invert already threadbare myths of American innocence into new myths of national depravity. The persistence of poverty seemed to confirm the turpitude of capitalism. The rapid decline of urban amenities, the rise of tawdry suburban tracts, the increasing incidence of crime, and the flouting of established codes of etiquette and courtesy all indicated the breakdown of community controls. Beyond these topical disorders, the residue of *Gemeinschaft* and Victorian restraint, which before mid-century had checked the advance of modernism, was losing its grip on the middle class.

Youth raised on a Disneyland version of the future had come of age to discover a complicated and brutal world. Many felt cheated. With outrage and ridicule, they turned on the bourgeois institutions and values with which their parents had provided them: family, church, work, patriotism, profit, achievement. In universities, learning and then echoing the often shopworn ideas of an earlier avant-garde, they denounced the middle class's hypocrisy, repressiveness, and immorality. Soon, doting and guilt-stricken adults, disturbed by war and deep social imperfections, joined the chorus. To vocal members of two generations shamed by their past, traditional America seemed out of date, if not a direct antecedent to My Lai. All had to be made anew!

43

And so it went with the schools, which, after all, trained the nation's youngest citizens.

With alarming frequency classroom teachers were encountering young nihilists, neo-Merovingians, fifteen-year-old shamans, and would-be Black Panthers and suffering a social climate that tended to reinforce all juvenile claims to moral monopoly. Even moderate students, and they always remained in the majority, were growing restive. When young people demanded that schools produce more relevant curriculums and pay more attention to their individual needs, educators raised on the thin diet of mid-century Progressive philosophy had few defenses. Now shamed by fashionable education critics and scorned by students, they reacted with confusion, hand-wringing, and guilt, in short, with failed nerve.

Trying to appease radicals of all stripes, educational leaders redoubled their reform efforts, creating new programs, abandoning strict standards of achievement, and giving militant egalitarians more power. To meet new "needs," they manufactured courses in drug, sex, moral, work, and consumer education. They gave students court-enforced "rights" and chased federal dollars to expand welfare services. They did everything except defend the integrity of the curriculum and a reasonable code of conduct.

The center was not holding. As many teachers grew bewildered or frightened, *au courant* educators learned new slogans. In innumerable faculty meetings, conferences, and high-level colloquiums, the chant went up: The school should concentrate on its students' personal development. It must expand its social responsibilities. Life adjustment redux! Daring yet again to build a new social order! Trendy opinion came wrapped in psychedelic colors and black armbands, perhaps. But in its soul, the New Age was Kilpatrick's and Counts's loyal grandchild, cut loose to present the decadent Progressive case in fevered and absolute terms.

Increasingly, the problem was a "liberal" definition of equality. Before 1965 Great Society planners had set out to reduce class and economic differences by increasing educational opportunities for low-income children and abolishing official forms of school discrimination. Supporting the concept of equal opportunity, they sought to eliminate obstacles to mobility that students encountered by reason of their social group or parent's wealth. They did not expect the educational system to make everyone equally competent or rich. But by inducing a better balance among social efficiency, individual liberty, and human equality, they argued, talent, energy, and excellence would be rewarded more fairly.

Other policy planners were less interested in the reward of merit than the quest for absolute equality. For such levelers, an equal chance to succeed was not enough. These egalitarians were more concerned that individuals receive equal amounts of income, status, and power through the redistributive mechanism of a state bureaucracy, even at the expense of individual liberty and incentives.

Americans have long glowed with faith in the alchemical properties of public "common" schools, at least since Horace Mann wrote in 1848, "Education, beyond all other devices of human origin, is the great equalizer of the condition of men—the balance wheel of the social machinery." The Great Society planners and implementers held quite the same views, though they were more enamored with the problem-solving powers of the federal government, the efficacy of bureaucratic reorganization, and the wisdom of court mandates. (And they were concerned with kinds of commonality—of race and viewpoint—that Mann had never considered.) For social reformers in the sixties, the schoolhouse was the place where the agonizing problems of crime, urban decay, and poverty intersected and could be remedied. Lack of education, after all, was the social variable most highly correlated with unemployment.

But then, just as the federal government and urban school boards started to pour huge amounts of money into compensatory programs for low-income students, fresh research contradicted these assumptions. Two landmark reports appeared. Both would have phenomenal impact on conventional wisdom about schools and education policy during the seventies. The first, which came out in 1966, was a massive equal educational opportunities survey, authorized by Congress in the Civil Rights Act two years earlier and later known as the Coleman Report, named for the study leader, James S. Coleman, a highly respected sociologist then at Johns Hopkins University. The second, an ambitious study of the impact of schools on economic inequality conducted by Christopher Jencks and other Harvard researchers, amplified the Coleman Report when it appeared in book form in 1972.

The Coleman Report surveyed about 650,000 students, 60,000 teachers and 4,000 schools across the nation. Early in the study, Coleman and his research team had little doubt about what they would eventually find: a "striking" difference between the quality of the school that the average black child attended and the one the average white child attended, thus accounting for the inferior achievement of minority students. But then, to Coleman's surprise, the findings controverted his hypothesis.

The Coleman Report held, first, that racially segregated schools remained widespread, which astonished almost no one. Then it found that minority children had serious educational deficiencies at the start of school, that they demonstrated lower average achievement levels than white pupils through all grades, and that the gap widened from the first through the twelfth grade. It also asserted, and this was crucial, that resource inequalities between black and white schools were not so great and that varying facilities such as libraries, laboratories, or gymnasiums, and even curricula or teachers had very little effect on student achievement. Coleman later wrote:

> Per pupil expenditure, books in the library, and a host of other facilities and curricular measures show virtually no relation to achievement if the "social" environment of the school—the educational background of other students and teachers—is held constant. Altogether, the sources of inequality of educational opportunity appear to lie first in the home itself and the cultural influences immediately surrounding the home; then they lie in the schools' ineffectiveness to free achievement from the impact of the home, and in the schools' cultural homogeneity which perpetuates the social influences of the home and its environs.

The importance of the Coleman Report, of course, lay in its confirmation of what many of us take for granted today: Academic outcomes depend in large part on the family background, peer group, and community values children bring to school, that minority students tend not to bring the proper baggage, and that "throwing money" at the schools attended by poor students does not magically alter their low attainments. To contemporaries the Coleman Report seemed to offer impressive evidence that the school was unable to shape society. And quickly the Coleman findings were reduced into an ill-considered motto: *Schools don't make a difference.*

This treacherous conclusion made all school curriculums, requirements, and policies seem equally unsatisfactory. It was a rabbit punch to superior curriculums and school practices. It also seemed to invalidate the activities of all dedicated teachers and administrators. Finally, it allowed any educational outlook to present itself as equally valid to any other and, no matter how bizarre or narrow, to present its particular philosophy or program as a possible educational salvation.

So arose a powerful concept, that the influences of a child's family, background, and peers were so potent that formal schooling had only minimal effect on cognitive development. And soon came a corollary: Educational reform could not penetrate the culture of poverty. Six years after the Coleman Report, Jencks's *Inequality* made this case most forcefully. Introduced at a Waldorf-Astoria press conference and given front-page coverage by *The New York Times,* the study was yet another blow to continuing educational efforts for poor and minority children—and to education itself. Jencks, a protégé of David Riesman, a former editor at *The New Republic,* and a researcher at the Institute for Policy Studies, had reanalyzed Coleman's data. His conclusion: Coleman had *underestimated* the importance of family background and other noneducational factors in determining student outcomes.

Infusions of government money, desegregation ventures, and compensatory programs, said Jencks, had no significant effect on reducing economic inequality. Even if all children could be made to do equally well in school, economic disparities would persist because of an individual's luck, personality, or on-the-job competence. According to this view, then, any reformer anxious to use the school as an instrument of economic betterment was doomed to bitter disappointment. "As long as egalitarians assume that public policy cannot contribute to economic equality directly, but must proceed by ingenious manipulation of marginal institutions like the schools, progress will remain glacial," Jencks concluded. Less than a decade after the enactment of the Elementary and Secondary Education Act, at least in the eyes of one powerful theoretician, the public school was not Mann's "balance wheel" but a "marginal institution." Suddenly the school's wonder-working reputation was collapsing.

Neither Coleman nor Jencks, of course, can be blamed for the gross oversimplifications of their findings. But in retrospect the damage was enormous. Both studies suggested to large numbers of professional educators and intellectuals that schools do not really have the power to do anything useful or important and that differences among schools are insignificant. For all the seventies, these popular notions undercut the idea that, of all social agencies, schools are best equipped to teach cognitive skills and that some schools do so much better than others. Jencks, appearing to despair of education's meliorative effects, proposed unprecedented federal activity either to make income supplements to the poor or to force employers to reduce the gap in wages between their best-paid and worst-paid workers. This was a prescription that amounted to, in Jencks's own word, socialism. After 1970, like others in the education establishment's advance guard, the Harvard *Wunderkind* was stepping beyond the outer limits of the new Progressivism, crossing the threshold into radical politics.

The historians were not far behind. By the early seventies a group of revisionist historians was painting a baleful portrait of the school as an American social institution, giving historical context to radical claims about the "repressive" contemporary school. The school's historical purpose, they suggested, had been to manipulate and control the working class as well as inculcate in the poor appropriate work habits of docility and obedience. Schools, then, were toady instruments through which plutocratic leaders conditioned youth to the industrial system and created a tractable U.S. labor force. Accordingly, compulsory school laws had been enacted to domesticate and "sort" youth from every quarter of society. The myth of school as a springboard of social mobility was a cruel hoax, they said, perpetuated by a capital-holding elite to stupefy the masses.

These were not liberals in a hurry. As Diane Ravitch has pointed out of radical scholarship in *The Revisionists Revised:*

> Where liberals had argued that the spread of public schooling was
> social progress, radicals saw the public school as a weapon of social

control and indoctrination; where liberals had maintained that reforms like compulsory schooling freed children from oppressive workplaces, radicals saw compulsory schooling as an expansion of the coercive power of the state; where liberals believed in the power of schooling to liberate people from their social origins, the radicals perceived the school as a social sorting device which undergirds an unjust, exploitative class system; where liberals considered the school to be an integral part of democratic society, radicals viewed it as a mechanism by which one group (an elite) exploits and manipulates another (the masses or the workers or the minorities or "the community"); where liberals had worked to insure that individual merit would be rewarded without regard to race or religion or other ascriptive factors, radicals described the outcome of this effort as meritocracy, hierarchy, and bureaucracy.

Given the Coleman Report and the rising tide of antischool literature, how to proceed on school reform became a burning topic among the best and the brightest. Students and professors in elite universities had already discovered Goodman, Kozol, and Neill. Some idealistic youths were entering teacher training programs to avoid the draft or remake the social contract "from the bottom up." College presidents, editorialists, foundation executives, social scientists, union leaders, and government and school officials, some of whom had been staunch guardians of traditional education in the past, became cheerleaders for massive government interventions and a cascade of "innovations." School principals, department heads, and teachers, inevitably responding to the clamor for change, were highly susceptible to the conflicting and grandiose remedies. Abruptly the sentiments of the moderate reigning elites were coalescing into a liberal consensus that seemed restrained beside the searing and relentless indictments of romantic and Marxist radicals.

In this climate these powerful individuals, anxious to appear educationally alert and up to date, sought an authoritative analysis of what was wrong with the schools and what adjustments were needed. In 1970 it came in Charles Silberman's *Crisis in the Classroom,* a comprehensive study four years in the making, sponsored by the Carnegie Corporation. For anyone trying to make sense of the fresh turmoil

49

in schools and then posit "liberal" solutions, the book was required reading. A former *Fortune* editor and author of the acclaimed *Crisis in Black and White,* Silberman had by common agreement produced a most intelligent, gripping, and well-argued case for profound educational redesign.

Many of the complaints registered in *Crisis in the Classroom* were already familiar. As Silberman saw it, U.S. schools continued to deny adequate resources and opportunities to low-income and minority children. They promoted formalism and student docility. They preferred tried-and-true curricula to more vital and interesting courses of study. The reform efforts of the fifties and sixties, Silberman concluded, voicing the prevailing liberal sentiment of the day, had amounted to little.

Even now, unlike the bulk of antischool literature churned out in the sixties and seventies, *Crisis in the Classroom* remains valuable and absorbing reading. Silberman's elucidation of the roots of schooling's crisis—that youth were questioning, rejecting, and at bottom failing to understand the authority of culture, morality, law, achievement, and truth—still holds. Concerned about all the educating institutions, including the electronic media, churches and synagogues, museums and libraries, armed forces and family, Silberman correctly viewed education as the business of the general public and not exclusively of educators.

But his prescriptions, it has turned out, were ill considered. To correct the defects of the schools, said Silberman, educationists must transform them into "free, open, humane and joyous institutions." They must overcome the system's core problem, *mindlessness,* which he defined as "the failure or refusal to think seriously about educational purpose, the reluctance to question established practice."

Today few of us would want to send our children to anything other than free, open, humane, and joyous institutions, as long as such places are not chaotic playgrounds where learning the basic subjects and habits of critical thinking is merely one of many equally valid alternative activities. Few of us would endorse mindlessness, in schools or anywhere else. But school analysts have spent a decade or more thinking seriously about every educational purpose and questioning every established practice. The process has often been lethal to estimable purposes and practices of the past. Silberman's word

50

mindlessness now looks like an intellectual's wrecking ball, capable of leveling fine, traditional constructions of education, worthy edifices sacrificed because their beaux-arts forms were temporarily out of fashion.

By way of remedy Silberman cited examples of particular schools offering what he considered to be valuable learning environments. At the primary level his examples—ranging from English infant schools to North Dakota elementary school science workshops—resembled the most thoughtful and effective "learning by doing" classrooms popular in progressive schools of the twenties and thirties.

At the secondary level Silberman espoused, too quickly, a cavalcade of innovations that ultimately had disastrous consequences for most of the institutions that embraced them. To Silberman, for example, one of the country's "lighthouse" high schools was Portland's John Adams High. Organized by a group from the Harvard Graduate School of Education and intended to act as a laboratory of experimental and enlightened school practices, it opened with a sleek physical plant and much community goodwill in September 1969. It offered the latest versions of peer counseling, independent study, work experience, pass–fail grading, interdisciplinary courses, and education-as-problem-solving. The curriculum for the first week was an intense schoolwide discussion of racial incidents that occurred on the opening day of school. Adam's young, suave faculty prided itself on how well it "related" to the student body.

Not long after Silberman's book appeared, though, the bubble burst. By the mid-seventies in Portland, Adams—a laughingstock of trendy methods, besieged by violence and white flight—epitomized the troubled progressive city school. Finally, in 1980, the city closed Adams for good on account of falling enrollments. By then virtually all of its charter faculty members had gone elsewhere. The principal had returned to Massachusetts and later held high-level jobs in the state and federal education bureaucracy.

Even more than Silberman, Charles Reich's *The Greening of America,* also published in 1970, reflected the cresting national orgy of youth worship. First serialized in *The New Yorker,* then a best-selling blockbuster, it became the most widely reviewed and discussed book on the counterculture then or since. Today the book would be

51

beneath notice, were it not so much a book of its times. According to Reich, a Yale law professor, the path to edenic happiness lay in the imitation of youth. The young would lead the way into a "green" land of freedom and naturalness, away from the parched and regimented technocratic state. So rode the spirit of *puer aeternus* across the land, Rousseau in the Sky with Diamonds.

Thus *The Greening of America's* significance: Its publication dates the moment when privileged youth's hedonistic cravings, slick putdown of the bourgeois world, and Dionysian revels became chic and "modern" attitudes, models for trend-conscious *adults*. Reich's screed attests to the real revolution of the late sixties and early seventies, which was not so much political or economic as cultural. A paean to antireason and preoccupation with self, the book anticipated the virulent social temper of our times.

FOUR

The Perils
of Benevolence

ROMANTIC VISIONARIES LIKE NEILL and Reich received exceptional publicity in the early seventies, for they represented a new view of youth shared increasingly by influential scholars, leading intellectuals, and cosmopolitan literary audiences. The counterculture had served up the young as models of innocence and moral rectitude. Fashionable notions were circulating: that adults had much to learn from children, that adult exertions on youth were coercive and possibly damaging, that a more permissive mode of life would emancipate the young *and* the old from suffocating bourgeois conventions.

Yet those dreaming the libertarian dream, increasingly detached from and neutral toward politics, paid little attention to the initiatives of other meliorists. Many government officials and education authorities were also affected by the spirit and slogans of emancipation. They, too, were intent on revising the nature of schooling. But their ideas of freedom usually had a less Rousseauan tint. With ambitious equity goals in mind, they leaned more and more heavily on the coercive capacities of legislative acts, executive regulations, and judicial orders, in other words, on the power of public policy to achieve dramatic social changes.

Today the remaining loyalists of once novel and now entrenched federal education programs are on the defensive. They point out that Washington's donations to the public elementary and secondary system have always amounted to a small portion of total education expenditures. And to be fair, it is correct that less than 10 percent of the nation's school revenues each year come from the federal treasury. But dollars contributed are not the central issue. Far more important since 1965 have been the kinds of education that Washington has chosen to purchase, the degree to which federal authorities and inspectors have seen the schools as centers of civil rights activities, what groups have been targeted for special financial and legal assistance, and what messages have been transmitted from Washington to state and local education agencies about the appropriate functions and responsibilities of public schools.

The Great Society policy-makers were highly educated instrumentalists, enamored of federal capabilities, who shaped new programs and policies with an eye toward redistributing educational resources, revising private conduct, and equalizing student outcomes. Their corps included advocacy lawyers, regulation writers, legislative assistants, political scientists, and grassroots organizers. These reformers grew in influence and consolidated their power by understanding the ways of the state and federal apparatus. They benefited from a spreading enthusiasm for national solutions and centralized policy. Unlike many local leaders, they were able to understand new protocols in state and federal government. They could comprehend complicated timetables, appropriation schedules, and regulatory minutiae. They were adept in litigating rights, practiced in scientific systems analysis, and zealous in presenting their activities as indisputable exercises of justice.

Increasingly these reformers represented organized interest groups and aggrieved individuals who found it more efficient to seek federal or state-level remedies than to lobby at the district level. Eventually their grand allies were the nation's courts, which in the seventies, according to Theodore H. White in *America in Search of Itself,* were "spraying the United States Constitution into every nook and cranny of national life, into matters best left to state legislatures, or into trivia that in other times might have been left to city halls or town councils." The federal presence intensified in the Nixon and Ford years. But by 1977, after the Carter Administration came to Washington, the new Progressives could count on a political climate ready to indulge their wildest demands. Congressional committees were fully sympathetic with their goals, regulation writers were willing to centralize education policy to an extent once thought impossible, and federal jurists were willing to ignore the schools' basic cognitive responsibilities in order to remake the educational system in line with liberal social doctrine.

Now, a list of the most ambitious battles won by liberal reformers in recent years bears testimony to the perils of benevolence, to new kinds of discrimination, to rotted relations between the generations, to the revolution of rising entitlements, and to the cynical self-interest of leading educational groups. Salient government initiatives have yielded, at best, an uneven harvest of benefits. Especially in cities, initiatives including those below have produced public antipathy and unforeseen social side effects—but few demonstrable improvements in learning.

DESEGREGATION

The complex issues of racial policy dominate federally based education activity. For almost thirty years desegregation—in schools and elsewhere—has been the most controversial article of national social planning. Nothing else has so well revealed federal capabilities to alter institutions in the face of private resistance. And arguably, nothing else has caused more social fractionation, especially in the places where orders *requiring integration* (often by group quotas) have succeeded orders *forbidding segregation* (and group discrimination).

Draconian desegregation measures evolved partly from bad faith and district-level intransigence after *Brown.* After 1960 Southeastern school boards, facing the glare of national publicity, found it impossible to resist integration efforts through violence and outright intimidation.

55

Instead they became masters of evasion and duplicity. To keep school-children of different races apart, dual school systems persisted, only with so-called freedom of choice. This meant, in effect, white students could attend black schools, which they did not, and black students could attend white schools, which few were brave or foolish enough to do.

Then came the Civil Rights Act of 1964. Title IV gave the Justice Department power to mount suits against segregated school districts. Title VI allowed the federal government to withhold funds from districts practicing segregation. Rapidly, crusading executive bureaucracies were set up to enforce the law. Their boldness produced successes. But many civil rights organizations, government officials, and district judges remained unsatisfied. Integrationists turned their attention from the Southeast to de facto segregation by neighborhood in Northern and Western cities. In the late sixties federal courts all over the country started to demand numerical evidence to prove that school integration was proceeding with more than deliberate speed.

Thus began the unhappy history of racial balance. In 1971, in *Swann* v. *Charlotte–Mecklenburg,* the Supreme Court upheld the use of elaborate transportation schemes to regroup the races in public schools. "But in busing to distant schools, white children were in effect being conscripted to create an environment which, it had been decided, was required to provide equality of opportunity for black children," the Harvard sociologist Nathan Glazer observed. The racial neutrality or "color-blindness" of *Brown* and the Civil Rights Act was being converted into a system of racially determined student school assignments, which Glazer concluded amounted to "as drastic a reduction of freedom as we have seen in this country in recent years." By the early eighties complicated and unstable codes in districts across the land tried to balance racial compositions of schools through zones, grades, magnets, pairings, clusterings, and a multitude of other ingenious techniques.

In 1982 an estimated total of 1.5 million schoolchildren were being bused for purposes of integration, as against 19 million for purposes of necessary travel to the nearest school. At least 720 school districts (including more than half of the nation's largest systems) operated under federal or state court orders; 1,200 others had created "voluntary" plans, sometimes negotiated under threat of suits and administrative sanctions, sometimes engineered to placate and forestall unhappy federal authorities.

At what cost? From the standpoint of social mixture and racial balance, at least in districts where a significant number of white children still remain in public schools, these plans have succeeded. But urban middle-class whites have resolutely refused to send their children to schools where most pupils are black or Hispanic. Why? The reason is class much more than racial friction. Working-class and middle-class parents of any race generally insist that their children attend school with classmates raised in families where scholastic achievement and good manners are prized. They will not willingly transfer their children from high-achieving to low-achieving or from safe to unsafe schools, even when the government orders them to do so. Furthermore, they bitterly resent government fiats that seem to imperil their own child's future in order to provide opportunities for other people's children.

Especially in metropolitan areas, the middle class has leaked from public school districts with large lower-class populations into private schools. More often it has moved to districts where real estate prices tend to protect bourgeois values in the public schools. As early as 1975 the sociologist James S. Coleman (whose 1966 equal educational opportunities survey had indicated that racial mixture would result in improved performance for black students and had been invoked frequently in behalf of new integration plans) had some bad news. He informed several powerful education groups that desegregation measures were contributing to a middle-class exodus—"white flight"—from city school districts. Coleman's observation touched off a firestorm of controversy, mainly refutations and denunciations of his claims. To many devoted integrationists these unpleasant findings were taken as evidence of Coleman's own apostasy and betrayal of the cause. Nonetheless, in most large municipalities today white public school enrollments have shrunk to such a low level that racial integration remains nothing more than a theoretical possibility.

And at times school management has become impossible. In 1980

57

the former Boston school superintendent, Robert D. Wood, registered his complaints as a beleaguered administrator in *The Wall Street Journal:* As the city's chief educational executive, he said, he was complying with more than 200 separate court orders; his system's legal bill the previous year had exceeded $700,000. According to Wood, the never ending rumors and gossip about the "will" of the federal court was the most insidious force in undermining his power and credibility.

Had all these problems persuaded the courts to consider other drives, including the pursuit of educational effectiveness before the enforcement of racial balance? The record is mixed. A significant 1983 decision in a federal district court approved a school desegregation plan for Chicago that abandoned the remedy of mandatory busing. But a Sixth Circuit Court of Appeals decision, affirming *Swann* as the law of the land, recently struck down a Nashville, Tennessee, plan explicitly designed to stem white flight, encourage neighborhood schools, and improve educational quality for children of all races.

For many inside and outside the courts in the early eighties, opposition to current initiatives in compulsory integration for any reason amounted to intransigent racism, however subtly expressed. "Clearly, court-ordered busing is alive and well," the Rand Corporation researcher David J. Armor said. "This is a remarkable achievement for perhaps the most unpopular, least successful, and most harmful national policy since Prohibition."

How desegregation and busing systems will evolve in coming years is not known. For some time integrationists have sought court mandates for interdistrict systems, which would encompass central cities and suburbs, thereby preventing the possibility of white flight. In an acrimonious 5–4 split, the Supreme Court in 1974 rejected in *Milliken* v. *Bradley* a lower court's interdistrict busing order for Detroit and fifty-three surrounding suburbs. Still, federal courts have approved such metropolitan plans in Louisville, Indianapolis, and Wilmington. In the Senate proposals to limit court busing powers have surfaced but stand little chance of quick enactment into law. The House and the Attorney General have recently instructed the Justice Department to cease pursuing court cases that could lead to the busing of students to adjust the racial composition of schools.

COMPENSATORY EDUCATION

Unlike busing, attempts to provide special educational help for children from low-income families enjoy broad-based public approval. In trying to give this assistance, Title I of the Elementary and Secondary Education Act has developed into the king of federal education categoricals. Since 1965 Title I has distributed more than $30 billion in grants to states and local districts to use in different ways to treat academic deficiencies, primarily at the elementary level. It now operates in about 14,000 districts and involves about 6 million children. Title I's efficacy has been the subject of much inconclusive research and debate. According to many recent studies, including a 1982 federal report that drew in part on National Assessment of Educational Progress findings and several convincing municipal surveys, Title I may provide modest academic benefits to disadvantaged youngsters.

The most penetrating objections to Title I arise from the ways in which it is organized. First, one must remember that, at the time of ESEA's passage, many district-level educators would have preferred federal assistance in the form of general grants for construction and salaries. But strict categorical targeting was more politically feasible. As a result, Title I programs were not grounded in sound and proven academic methods. Second, the Title I idea reflected enormous faith in social science and the value of improved educational materials. Therefore, monies have gone either to increase the ranks of specialists, aides, diagnosticians, and psychologists or to provide new machinery and equipment. The emphasis has been on overcoming student "deficiencies," not on improving the quality of teachers and the curriculum. And in some cases Title I has developed into a pork-barrel jobs program, especially for the parents of minority children, given employment under the guise of community participation.

Quality control is Title I's first problem. In some districts several different experimental remedial programs operate side by side, without any regard to effectiveness or grade-to-grade continuity. Sometimes a child will encounter several remedial efforts that contradict one another. Paul Copperman, president of the Institute of Reading Development, also raises questions about Title I's externalities. Being "pulled out" of regular classes to attend special remedial sessions, he argues, is disruptive and increases classroom confusion. Bringing an army of outside specialists into the learning process may undercut the authority of the regular teacher, he adds. Other researchers have asserted that Title I specialists (like other "special" educators) tend to have nonlocal loyalties. Their interests, instead, tend to be vertical, that is, running from school to district office to state agency to federal department, at the expense of a horizontal layer of faculty fellowship and collegial unity.

This last point suggests Title I's huge political constituency, which in some poor districts can exert a flying-wedge presence in local policymaking. Program administrators, special staff and parent aides all derive their salaries from the federal government. As a result, they can sometimes ignore the wishes of local superintendents and principals. Similarly, they have a distinct interest in promoting the current style of compensatory education, no matter what its impact on schools or on children. Under present federal regulations, in fact, Title I educators have a vested interest in the persistence of learning disabilities: If all children in a Title I school were to begin magically to work at grade level, after a year's grace period the school would lose by law its extra faculty positions and special materials.

BILINGUAL EDUCATION

Fifteen years ago the idea seemed to be a humane and appealing alternative to thrusting large numbers of Hispanic, Asian and Indian children into "sink or swim" classrooms where no provision had been made for their lack of fluency in English. "Transitional" bilingual education, it was said, would provide students with two languages, preventing children who spoke little or no English from falling behind in other subjects while they learned English vocabulary, grammar, and composition. So in 1968 Congress appropriated a tiny $8 million for bilingual demonstration programs that states and cities might later adopt and pay for themselves.

Then, in 1974, aware of rising linguistic tensions in the schools, the Supreme Court in *Lau* v. *Nichols* required local districts to make some special instructional allowances for students struggling in schools because they did not speak English. (The court did not mandate a specified "bilingual" system.) In the so-called *Lau* remedies issued the following year, the Office for Civil Rights in the Department of Health, Education, and Welfare promulgated guidelines that emphatically prescribed the use of the "home language" in schools, even those with a small concentration of students whose primary language was not English. OCR also identified several hundred school districts (most of them very large) said to be in violation of *Lau* v. *Nichols.*

Henceforth, any school district independent, experimental, or uncooperative enough to employ special provisions other than those recommended by the Office for Civil Rights risked having all its federal funding terminated. And to those in HEW's regional offices this was no idle threat. For many local school officials in the mid-seventies, the *Lau* remedies turned into a bureaucratic nightmare. In 1977, for example, 222 districts were declared in "noncompliance" with the Civil Rights Act on account of their programs for students not able to speak English and ordered to submit corrective plans. *New York Times* education correspondent Gene Maeroff recorded one amazing HEW directive to the Saginaw, Michigan, school superintendent that ordered the local staff to identify students in need of assistance more sensitively through the following system:

> Determine—by observation—the language used by the student to communicate with peers between classes or in informal situations. The assessments must cross-validate one another (example: student speaks Spanish at home and Spanish with classmates at lunch). Observers must estimate the frequency of use of each language spoken by the student in these situations. In the event that the language determinations conflict (example: student speaks Spanish at home, but English with classmates at lunch), an additional method must be employed by the District to make such a determination (for example, the district may wish to employ a test of language dominance as a third criterion).

At the same moment some leading bilingual education advocates openly rejected the "transitional" approach. Other languages, they said, should not be mere bridges into English instruction. Instead the emphasis should be on "bicultural" school programs and "mainte-

61

nance" of the student's home language and ethnic identity. This was an outlook that Noel Epstein, the *Washington Post* education editor, in a distinguished review of bilingual education, called "affirmative ethnicity."*

In the movement for affirmative ethnicity, militant Chicanos and Puerto Ricans led the way, for more than 80 percent of bilingual programs were aimed at Spanish-speaking youngsters. Such programs struck—and strike—at the English language as a national instrument of communication and an agent of ethnic assimilation. In some places young Hispanics and other students are denied the right to learn English, kept in high school level bilingual classes long after they have learned enough English to enter regular classrooms.

To some education officials this amounts to a form of segregation, usually voluntary, that may ultimately force such students to endure the same marginal existence that their parents have faced. But according to some ethnic separatists such classes are a purifying step toward group consciousness and away from the oppression, delusion, and outdated concept of an American commonwealth. At least $130 million in federal funds and more from state governments means that on the fate of bilingual education ride many jobs. And Albert Shanker, president of the American Federation of Teachers, is one of many who complain that these special monies provide employment for badly educated Spanish-speaking teachers who would normally be ineligible for standard certification.

For a nation to provide large federal and state subsidies to create and then sustain education programs encouraging linguistic divisions is very questionable public policy. At the moment bilingual education's popularity at the federal level is on the wane. And with reason. Even transitional bilingual education programs are not fully effective, according to a 1977 evaluation of bilingual education conducted by the American Institutes for Research and a 1981 survey by the U.S. Department

---

* Some extremists sought students of other ethnic backgrounds to round out bicultural classes. One recalls a chilling photograph in a 1977 issue of *Newsweek* magazine. A tiny San Francisco black girl, perhaps in the second grade, evidently tries to identify the Chinese character for "room." In another case, a Vietnamese refugee in a Chicago high school protested, in English, when his teacher insisted on speaking Spanish in his mathematics class. He was ridiculed—and subsequently ignored—by the instructor.

of Education. Some studies suggest that the widely discredited "immersion" system, when sensitively applied, does result in marked student progress. And yet, especially in states including California, Texas, and Florida, with huge concentrations of Spanish-speaking residents, fierce sentiment favoring bilingual-bicultural education lingers on—along with ethnic strife and the threat, should such programs be halted, of political strife.

EDUCATION OF THE HANDICAPPED

To almost everyone, the concept of increasing educational access and opportunities for handicapped students represents an advanced state of civic sensibility. Two federal acts, the Rehabilitation Act of 1973 and the Education for All Handicapped Children Act of 1975, have signaled these public responsibilities to all school districts. The problem is degree and cost. Who qualifies as disabled? Who, then, is entitled to "special" education? And at what price for equipment and services?

The laws require free and appropriate education, special classes for some, "mainstreaming" for others, but equal opportunity for all disabled children. When possible, the goal is integration of the handicapped into regular classrooms. But educational access can require schools to modify their physical plants to accommodate the movements and needs of anyone blind, deaf, or crippled. Since the disabled need machinery and specialists to enjoy full access, school programs should also provide, for example, elevators, books in braille, or sign-language teachers. According to law, school and parent must agree on an Individual Education Plan (IEP) for every disabled youngster. If parents do not care for the school diagnosis, they may go to another medical authority, who may then propose an alternative IEP.

This is all very expensive, especially when educational problems become tangled with severe medical pathology. The average cost of educating a handicapped child is at least twice that of an ordinary student. This financial burden would be an enlightened and just public expense, if the definitions of "handicapped" and "school responsibility" were not almost boundless. A student's right to special education is by no means confined to the mentally retarded and physically disabled.

It extends to disabilities not clear-cut, such as hearing impairment, minimal brain dysfunction, or social maladjustment.

Who is handicapped? Across the country, *more than 4 million* IEPs were written in the academic year 1978–79. And federal promises to contribute a large share of the cost to fulfill these plans have not been kept.

Before 1982 the federal courts interpreted the educational rights of the handicapped very expansively. One early and important case in a Pennsylvania district court declared the right of "appropriate education" to mean one that aims for every handicapped child's "self-sufficiency" and "maximum" potential. But if advanced technology, special services, and trained specialists are extended to one out of every ten students in public schools, local officials have argued, the costs will be staggering and unbearable. To comply with federal mandates for the handicapped, they have said, districts will be forced to compromise their regular programs.

Then, last year, in a split decision, the Supreme Court modified the right of appropriate education from one that entitles each handicapped child to "an opportunity to achieve his full potential" to a public education from which each child can derive "some educational benefit." Some saw this as a setback for the handicapped. But for others it seemed a balanced decision in line with new awareness of limited school resources.

Nonetheless, problems persist. Could it be that eligibility for special education has been defined too broadly, and often by self-interested specialists? Could "learning disabled" be nothing more than a new euphemism to justify the placement of minority children in classes where no learning takes place? Could it be that ambitious middle-class parents too readily resort to handicapped labels to explain away embarrassing shortcomings in their children's motivation or character? These remain unanswered questions.

STUDENT RIGHTS

For all the century state courts had upheld the principle of *in loco parentis* in schools so that authorities could carry out their stated responsibility to educate students in tax-supported institutions. Then, in the sixties, civil libertarians discovered the concept of children's rights and took their claims to the federal courts. In 1969, with a phrase as powerful—and potentially destructive—as a lightning bolt, the Supreme Court declared in *Tinker* v. *Des Moines* that "students [do not] shed their constitutional rights at the classroom door."

Schools have never been the same. A series of First and Fourteenth Amendment cases following *Tinker* introduced a new, revolutionary contractual relationship between adults and children in schools. For many federal judges and legal scholars in the seventies *in loco parentis* came to be perceived as nothing more than a trump card to deny young people many of the individual rights that adults took for granted.

An example in point is the University of California law professor Leon Letwin's exhaustive review of student due process rights in a 1977 issue of the *Stanford Law Review.* Letwin considered several arresting viewpoints questioning the wisdom of the new legal model of authority for schools: that children are weak, uninformed, and lacking in self-control, and therefore need protection by paternalistic authorities; that adversarial mechanisms are inappropriate in the benign setting of school, where the experience, good faith, and dedication of school staffs safeguard student interests; that denial of some rights is the quid pro quo for a student's privileged status outside the labor force; that a measure of student deference to adult will is indispensable to mental and moral growth; that "student rights" wave a red flag to the very pupils who need discipline the most; that courts might displace school officials as the supreme arbiters of the differences in the educational community; and that the "constitutionalization" of the teacher–pupil relationship could injure that emotional bond. Letwin rejected the validity of all these claims.

But Letwin and others underestimated the impact of expanded student freedom and rights on the school's climate. Just as public schools inherited new and onerous burdens to create a more equal and just society, their authority to enforce strict standards of student conduct was in part removed. This situation dramatically altered the psychological reality in which educators and students interacted. It stimulated an adversarial relationship between apprehensive adults and empowered children, in which legal mechanisms replaced customary ways of settling intergenerational conflicts. The public school climate necessarily became more tense, formal, and litigious.

Within a decade after *Tinker* many public schools, at least on the secondary level, published codes of student rights and disciplinary procedures detailed enough to satisfy a sea lawyer. All student behavior, unless specifically declared illegal, was regarded as tolerable. To "protect" students from teachers and principals, special child advocates in some districts monitored school discipline proceedings. Some district review and appeals boards could countermand the "arbitrary" decision of any principal. And the never distant threat of lawsuits made most school officials squirm at—or refuse to take—punitive action against even very disruptive or defiant students, especially if the administration was white and the student body nonwhite. Legal constraints on educators and the collateral hesitancy of adults in schools to enforce institutional rules became widely shared items of knowledge among young people. The most cynical of these students concluded correctly that no matter how annoying or depraved their conduct, school officials could not in practice deny them the "right" to go to school.

TESTING

In 1979 a U.S. district court in California ruled that the use of intelligence tests to place black children in classes for the educable mentally retarded violated the Fourteenth Amendment's equal protection clause. California's system for identifying students with learning disabilities had been selecting disproportionately more black than white children. "An unbiased test that measures ability or potential should yield the same pattern of scores when administered to different groups of people," Judge Robert F. Peckham declared. He then ordered the state to find a system that would produce black and white slow learners in numbers that matched the proportion of blacks and whites in the general population. The same year Congress and at least fourteen state legislatures were considering bills that would require test-makers to offer the contents of their examinations for public inspection. The

National Education Association had begun a campaign to abolish all standardized testing in public schools.

Perhaps this was just desert for test-makers once known for their arrogant claims of near-infallible precision. Even earlier the education scholar George Weber had cautioned against the misuse of tests, when they replace flexible human judgments about the instructional needs of individual pupils or track students into narrow and possibly permanent educational channels. Christopher Jencks and others make the valuable observation that schools should put more emphasis on achievement than on aptitude tests, since the former reflect mastery of the curriculum and reward those who actually learn. And, to its credit, the antitesting movement drew attention to the possibility that some standardized test questions might favor children who were more familiar with standard English speech or who had grown up in middle-class environments.

The case against tests is based on several premises: that standardized tests do not measure analytical or reasoning abilities of the kinds that most schools try to teach; that they are psychologically damaging and not worth their price in human suffering; that they are discriminatory to minority and low-income students; and that, being cognitive measures alone, they are narrow, barren, or invalid indices of human worth and creativity.

While each of these premises contains the grain of truth to make it a point of argument, most test critics in fact appear evasive about their central objection to all forms of standardized tests: General intelligence, aptitude, and achievement tests make distinctions of individual ability and performance. Tests rank students on qualities other than effort, character, or motivation; to deny that such cerebral qualities can be evaluated and ranked reduces the possibility of calling attention to human inequalities. This becomes a special problem when, on average, minority students do poorly on standardized tests, notwithstanding an authoritative 1982 report of the National Academy of Sciences that concluded that standardized tests are valid measuring instruments and not in themselves unfair to minorities.

To parents fearful for their children's future, people worried about the image of minority groups, and radical egalitarians, then, the evaluation of mental ability or scholastic attainment is a basic threat. Tests register the varying capabilities of individuals. They reflect all too well the difficulties that minority children face in learning and in achieving school success. To avoid these realities, some would like to put an end to meaningful student measurement. But, as the black psychologist Kenneth Clark said to *Newsweek* in 1980, this activity is like crushing the thermometer to avoid trying to cure the fever.

THE RISE OF THE SPECIAL INTERESTS

The local power of school boards, superintendents, and principals diminished rapidly during the seventies, first on account of nonlocal government initiatives, and second on account of local confusion over school aims. This was a dual trend that aided many national education associations. As topical issues such as those just described were debated, some well-established groups like the NAACP Legal Defense and Education Fund found that single-minded expertise gave them an incalcuable advantage in argument. Newly active associations such as the Council for Exceptional Children, the National Association for Career Education, and the American Council of Sex Educators, Counselors, and Therapists swiftly amassed great influence in setting their own field's agenda. Lobbying legislative staffs and education offices, they discovered, was easier than dealing in local school politics. In addition, federal- and state-level policy-makers were more likely to be ideologically sympathetic—or at least more insulated from the majoritarian politics of local government. When legislative committees met, the associations were ready with testimony, policy statements, and model regulative guidelines or laws. When any single program or appropriation they sought was buried, defeated, or vetoed, their representatives stood by to make dire charges in the press or take steps for court redress.

Of all the educational interest groups, the National Education Association achieved the most power, not least by acting as an umbrella organization for lesser councils, funds, and activists. During the first sixty years of the century the NEA had been a relatively quiet confederation of professional educators. It issued well-respected reports, retained amiable relations with school boards, and shied away from noneducational controversies. By comparison, the American Federation of Teachers' unionism seemed bumptious and vulgar. Still, in the sixties the NEA was threatened and shamed by the more energetic AFT, which gained urban districts by explicitly emulating the strategies of the industrial unions to gain new contractually based teacher protections and benefits.

Suddenly put on the defensive, the NEA copied the AFT's litigious and belligerent posture. In 1968 it ended its long-standing opposition to the teacher's use of the strike weapon. And in its conversion the NEA felt obliged to break with its bland and bipartisan past. The NEA had championed Progressive causes since the days of the *Cardinal Principles,* but it had always remained at the margin of national politics. Then, at the start of the seventies, the NEA national office acted with zeal to represent the many groups then feeling unserved by the public schools on account of race, gender, native language, physical disability, or institutional conventions. Soon the NEA became an ardent organized advocate of items such as compulsory busing, affirmative action, Title IX, bilingual education, mainstreaming of the handicapped, student rights, and experimental courses.

Quite early the NEA discerned the new political opportunities for a well-organized vertical association like itself, with offices in Washington and state capitals. By 1980, 1,500 professional field organizers gave it a cohesive chain of command reaching from the Potomac to individual schools. With about 1.6 million members in 9,000 district affiliates, the NEA reached into most American communities.

By 1972 President Catherine Barrett made the NEA's revised aims explicit: "We are the biggest potential striking force in this country and we are determined to control the direction of education," she said. As it turned out, that was merely the beginning. By 1978 NEA Executive Director Terry Herndon said, "We want leaders and staff with sufficient clout that they may roam the halls of Congress and collect votes to reorder the priorities of the United States of America."

Year by year the NEA's Washington-based leadership spent more time and members' dues campaigning for sympathetic political candidates. Instead of campaigning for better education, it became heavily committed to partisan, divisive, and essentially noneducational issues such as speedy nuclear disarmament, reduced defense spending, Third

World resistance to alleged imperialism by multinational corporations, equalization of worker earnings, abortion rights, and gun control.

During the presidential campaign in 1976 NEA leaders saw what seemed to be a certain chance to secure their hegemony in education affairs. A well-publicized NEA endorsement and mobilization helped an unknown former governor named Jimmy Carter to be elected President. In return the NEA put the squeeze on the Administration to consolidate the many social programs located in the public schools in a federal department.

Even at the beginning the wisdom of reorganizing national education activities was debated. Editorials in *The New York Times, The Wall Street Journal, The Washington Post,* and *The Chicago Tribune* attacked the proposal. Many legislators saw the venture as an ill-advised challenge to localism in school organization. Only 34 percent of teachers themselves thought that a department of education would have a positive impact on public school quality.

But led by the NEA, a coalition of groups benefiting from federally funded categorical programs outwitted the critics. In September 1979 the Department of Education's consolidating act squeaked through the House 215–201, in part because the White House turned the vote into an angry loyalty test for Democratic representatives. The night before President Carter signed the bill into law, on October 16, a top NEA official toasted: "Here's to the only union that owns its own Cabinet department." By then the NEA's power brokerage had become a study in greed and hubris.

Toward the end of the seventies the NEA national officers steadfastly supported new *Lau* regulations mandating a national curriculum based on "maintenance" and ethnic consciousness. They called standardized tests "similar to narcotics" for "maiming" children's minds. They identified U.S. militarism as a primary source of juvenile alienation and violence. They distributed inflammatory curricular materials, especially on the subject of race and racism,* prescribed for use in schools.

---

* A 1973 NEA manual designed for classroom use, *Education and Racism,* declared: "All white individuals in our society are racists. Even if whites are totally free from all conscious racial prejudices, they remain racists, for they receive benefits distributed by a white racist society through its institutions."

Today it is not only that the "successful schooling of children has steadily receded in the universe of NEA concerns," as Chester E. Finn, Jr., has observed. Too often the NEA plays the role of defender of mediocrity and national despair. "You can't put teachers up on pedestals in a decadent society," the NEA's Herndon said in a 1980 interview. "Teachers refuse to live a different standard in communities that expect them to teach children how to be better in the future."

The NEA is still smarting from its setbacks in the 1980 elections. For one thing, the Republican victories in the White House and Congress that year suggested that the teachers' union had less "clout" than some national politicians had been led to believe. For another, it suddenly ended the NEA's push for policy control in the federal department. Still, NEA activity has continued unabated in the statehouses, with notable agitation in behalf of the Equal Rights Amendment. Since the failure of ERA national officials have turned their attention to nuclear disarmament, leading a peace coalition called Citizens Against Nuclear War. In the 1982 congressional elections NEA political action committees gave $1.3 million to what they called "pro-education" candidates for the House and Senate, four times as much as in 1980.

So far the NEA's dominant outlook seems insensible to popular interest in educational productivity, neutral to intellect, and either apathetic or hostile to the advancement of values such as individual prudence and civic pride. Even to some middle-of-the-road observers, the NEA—in contrast to the rival AFT, which has registered increasing alarm over unsatisfactory school practices—has become the nation's most formidable organized obstacle to the restoration of learning.

What went wrong? Why did estimable public policy goals, in the opinion of many who once welcomed centralization and the federal aura in local schools, give way to practices detrimental to the process that they were intended to improve?

It should be obvious to critics that policies created for and adopted by a $100 billion enterprise—elementary and secondary education spending in the United States approximates the gross national product of India or Sweden—cannot develop in a pristine environment. It

71

should be just as obvious that the semi-autonomy of 16,000 governing boards will result in national education policies that undergo metamorphosis between the Potomac and Main Street. "The translation of federal programs to local setting does not resemble a precision drill team marching in order toward a specific goal or even an orderly bilateral negotiation," educational researcher Eleanor Farrar has said. Any change in education policy is subject to multiform pressures; innumerable classroom variations; and human passions, prejudices, errors, and follies. The educational process cannot be fully systematized.

Yet in quest of equality, sixties- and seventies-style reformers tried to do just so. That is where their problems began. Previously the federal government had provided a logical and benign source of leadership and money to like-minded reformers in state governments, district offices, public-interest organizations, and individual schools. Then, toward the end of the sixties, bold educational initiatives were reexamined and found to be halfhearted correctives. Policies instated after *Brown* v. *Topeka* were no longer sufficient. Driven by a guilty and wishful egalitarianism, the liberal consensus felt obliged to go faster and farther, even if much of the nation's school clientele disliked what it was doing.

A dozen years or so ago certain facts of education embarrassed "moderate" authorities: Schools could not countervail all family inequalities; schools, given differences of individual intelligence, could not equalize all student attainments; schools could not be entirely free and democratic institutions as long as adults convey knowledge and youngsters absorb it. So mortified, educational leaders endorsed new rounds of equalizing interventions and truckled to groups organized to represent the accredited (and virtuous) victims of (an unjust and culpable) society. No matter that the debate over the schools' academic and moral duties to the culture ground to a halt. No matter either that educators with serious qualitative concerns came to be seen as hopelessly elitist, probably racist, and certainly odd.

The federal government and increasingly imitative state agencies have begun to make policy in countless areas once reserved to local school boards, and not with a light touch. Federal solutions tend to have continental impact. To solve an educational problem state authorities invariably impose their solution on all the schools in the state. More than a thousand congressionally authorized education and training programs now exist. Who knows the additional number authorized by fifty state legislatures? Each of these programs has its own procedures, requirements, accountability standards, and protective bureaucracies. Appropriations for them total billions of dollars each year in salaries.

Incremental bureaucratic accretion has occurred at all government levels, resulting in what the Rand Corporation education scholar Arthur E. Wise has called the "hyperrationalization" of elementary and secondary education. This mode of management has tried to establish rules and procedures, to adopt scientific management practices, to specify goals in measurable outcomes, to inspect for compliance, to reduce local discretion, and to suspend individual judgment. In the effort to ensure equality and erase different school outcomes, the aim has been to advance and perfect the age-old ideal of the common school. Increasingly, though, it seems that the constitutional and programmatic revisions of the seventies have had precisely the opposite effect. And bureaucratic, centralized systems, once established and staffed, have proved themselves extremely skilled at resisting any external attempts to modify or rescind even their most ill-advised initiatives.

FIVE

The Changing World of Childhood

Uɴsᴀᴛɪsғᴀᴄᴛᴏʀʏ sᴄʜᴏᴏʟ ᴄʟɪᴍᴀᴛᴇs cannot be described as fully the consequence of mistaken educational ideas and public policies. With the confirmation of social science we may now heed what many wise people have known since the beginning of time: School inputs do not equal educational outcomes. External social forces exert claims of their own to forge a child's intellect and disposition. And today the quest for high educational attainments is complicated by the receding ability of authorities to uphold and enforce traditional values. Community schools face a thickening web of community customs, amusements, and values that add to their burdens, exacerbate their problems, and make their essential cognitive tasks harder to carry out.

The best educational policies in the world can be bruised by unsavory social conditions. If the civil situation is lax or unwholesome, schools cannot be expected to correct it singlehanded. And in the American culture, as the sociologist Robert K. Merton observed in an interview, "the forces of social decomposition may now outweigh the forces of composition." Three interconnected kinds of social dis-

74

junction now cut at hopes for the rapid expansion of disciplined schools. First, broken bonds of family and belief increase the school's caretaking responsibilities, while a lack of moral consensus reduces its force as an effective custodian. Second, generational roles and privileges are confused, mainly as a result of widespread adult insecurity. Third, fractured behavioral norms tend to level the distinctions of what is good and what is bad, depriving children of stable ethical models and making the standards of juvenile conduct ever more self-originated.

This is not to say that the force of disintegrative tendencies falls equally on all youth. Quite the opposite, in fact. Some young people experience adult negligence, relativism, anxiety, narcissism, and mendacity firsthand and acutely. Others are only vaguely aware that some of their classmates live quite differently from themselves—and more daringly. Yet the public school is expected to tolerate all styles of living, to take a "pluralistic" stance. As mores become less similar and as children's mores diverge from exemplary adult models, the schools try unsuccessfully to accommodate as equal outlooks that are adversarial. The consequence is often galloping institutional friction and some slippery official form of value-neutrality.

What is taking place is a multigenerational polarization of manners, which has important implications for education. The University of Michigan psychologist Joseph Adelson has put the matter plainly. More than any other institution in American society, he has observed, the schoolyard is the place where cultural traditionalism and modernism now struggle for the minds and hearts of the young. It is where values of "merit, accomplishment, competition, and success; self-restraint, self-discipline, and the postponement of gratification; the stability of the family; and a belief in moral universals" collide with a modern ethos that "scorns the pursuit of success; is egalitarian and redistributive in emphasis; tolerates or encourages sensual gratification; values self-expression as against self-restraint; accepts alternative or deviant forms of the family; and emphasizes ethical relativism."

Since mid-century, Adelson asserts, the reigning elites in the major universities, the foundations, the media, and the educational trade associations have consistently championed modernity, especially as it pertains to juvenile freedom. Out of intense desire to seem alert, open-minded, and enlightened, leading educators have acceded to such ideas. In contrast, most parents have expected schools to make their children literate, ambitious, and well-behaved. As a result of these conflicting goals, many educators have resorted to a kind of double-dealing. As educational planners rhapsodize and advance modernity, schools themselves try to appear faithful to traditional values. Adelson continues:

> It has not quite worked, not really. If you are going to hold children to high standards of achievement, you cannot at the same time, secretly, feel that ambition is a crass or ignoble motive. If you are going to teach children to be virtuous—that is, to be brave and loyal and honest—you must yourself possess a strong sense of what is right and wrong, and you cannot in one silent part of your mind feel that there are no moral absolutes, that virtue and vice are meaningless since they are understood differently among the Kwakiutl.

This ethical ambivalence, Adelson contends, helps to explain the schools' scrambled sense of mission and declining community reputation.

In their confusion, Adelson suggests, educational reformers have promised much more than they could deliver. With great flourish, they have introduced countless educational novelties, each one supposed to rectify a certain social misery and advance individual fulfillment. In the process, he believes schools have in fact given up ground to social influences that make them less friendly, purposeful places.

ALTERED BONDS OF ASSOCIATION

A revealing table appeared almost casually in a recent scholarly journal (Table 5–1). Reproduced below, it is a composite of 18 major studies ranking the force of various authorities on U.S. adolescents in 1960 and 1980. If we are to believe it, the changing influences on youth during these twenty years are nothing short of astonishing. Of ten authority groups, five lost ranking as forces shaping youthful attitudes: parents, teachers, clergy, youth leaders, and relatives. During the same

TABLE 5-1

Estimated Shifts in the Order of Influences on Youths Thirteen to Nineteen Years Old that Change Their Behavior

	1960	1980	
1	Mother, father	*Friends, peers*	(+2)
2	Teachers	Mother, father	(−1)
3	Friends, peers	*Television, radio, records, movies*	(+5)
4	Ministers, priests, rabbis	Teachers	(−2)
5	Youth club leaders, counselors, advisers, scoutmasters, coaches, librarians	*Popular heroes, idols in sports and music*	(+1)
6	Popular heroes, idols in sports and music	Ministers, priests, rabbis	(−2)
7	Grandparents, uncles, aunts	*Newspapers, magazines*	(+2)
8	Television, records	*Advertising*	(+2)
9	Newspapers, magazines	Youth club leaders, counselors, advisers, scoutmasters, coaches, librarians	(−4)
10	Advertising	Grandparents, uncles, aunts	(−3)

Source: Reprinted by permission of *Daedalus,* Journal of the American Academy of Arts and Sciences, Fall 1981, Cambridge, MA.

period five other groups gained ranking: friends, electronic media, popular heroes, print media, and advertising. Of the waning influences, the authority of nonparental counselors fell most dramatically. Of waxing influences, the forces of television, radio, records, and movies advanced most rapidly.

These findings are not encouraging. Once again, they confirm a continuing, possibly inexorable erosion of familiar adult and community power in the lives of the young. Parents unquestionably remain the most potent authority over small children and even many teenagers. But just as we know how much families count in effective schooling, their influence is diminishing. More and more young people rely— out of necessity or choice—on other associations and mechanisms to learn the ways of the world. Parents and local adults have a smaller place in the lives of the young, and newly dominant forces on children include the vulgar and trivial images produced by remote, invisible technicians and publicists, experts at spectacle creation, who are in the lucrative business of manufacturing tantalizing fantasies.

No longer can the weakened condition of the traditional nuclear family, less secure than at any time in memory, come as unexpected news. Still, family trends should alarm all who believe that directive mom-and-pop homes tend to coexist with, reinforce, and promote effective schools. They should dismay all who worry about rising rates of parental neglect. Between 1970 and 1979 traditional U.S. households—that is, those consisting of husband, wife, and at least one child, all living together—became a minority social institution. In other words, citizens who did not live within such households outnumbered those who did. At least one out of three marriages now ends in divorce, triple the rate in 1960. And among people under thirty—the trend-setters and parents of small children—the rate has quadrupled during the same period. In 1990, it is estimated, only slightly more than one-quarter of U.S. households will consist of married couples with children. Almost one out of two school-age children will live in a single-parent home, usually on account of divorce. (Before 1965 most children who lived in single-parent homes did so because of parental death.)

Of course, the decline of the traditional parent–child relationship can be easily overestimated. Some unconventional family networks perform admirably. American expectations for family life in terms of joy, comfort, and intimacy may be excessively high. But the commitment of citizens to families is persistent, the sociologist Mary Jo Bane has pointed out, mainly because families satisfy unabated "human needs for stability, continuity, and nonconditional affection." They are not, she says, "archaic remnants of a disappearing traditionalism." Nor is it possible, she concludes, for public faculties to replace the unique kinds of parental care.

Still, other forces militate against the family's ancient nurturing role. About 55 percent of all mothers with children under eighteen now work outside the home, usually to provide needed family income, a pressure that usually obviates the question, *Should a wife work?* In the professional and managerial classes feminist consciousness has altered, perhaps permanently, the status of homemaking and childrearing. To questionable benefit, many college-educated women who desire to be full-time housewives and mothers are likely to regard themselves as victims of social conditioning. And lest we forget, the workplace now offers many able women genuinely satisfying alternatives to homemaking.

Fairly or unfairly, parenthood has become less appetizing to the middle class. Childrearing is now perceived to be full of risks, a matter of financial deprivation for parents and possible emotional injury for their children. The Norman Rockwell–style images that once made family life so appealing have lost their luster and credibility. For many young adults in their twenties and thirties, as a consequence, the prospect of marrying and having children is not likely to provoke a sense of pleasurable anticipation. Between 1960 and 1980 the national birth rate declined by 40 percent to an all-time record low, followed by a very modest upturn.

At least for lower-class minorities family conditions are in fact dire. Over the last twenty years the proportion of black female-headed households has almost doubled from 23 to 41 percent of all black families. A majority of black children are now born out of wedlock. Since 1967 transgenerational clients of Aid for Families with Dependent Children—those who were reared on such welfare assistance and later became AFDC recipients themselves—have risen from about 20 to 40 percent.

With increasing frequency, poor and nonwhite children are being born to abandoned or unmarried, immature and ill-educated child-women. These single mothers rarely have the financial and mental wherewithal to give their children much more than affection. For many of these demoralized and ill-prepared mothers, survival literally depends on the support of their extended family or, more likely, on transfer payments and other tax-supported largesse. For their children, inevitably, the school's function as a welfare center—an institution

79

providing baby-sitting services, medical checkups, calories, and heat—overwhelms its function as a learning center.

When children of any social class are deprived of strong family ties, it would be reasonable to expect them to seek increased contact with exemplary adults. But this cannot be assumed in places where neighborhood ties tend to be weak (e.g., in suburban tract developments) or available adult models tend to be malign (e.g., in slums). In most communities today one child may grow up nurtured by benign adult counselors, including godparents, coaches, or local busybodies. Another child, living a few doors away, may grow up almost entirely estranged from adults. This second child might have to move every two or three years from an "old" neighborhood because of parental difficulties with marriage, jobs, or finances. By adolescence such a child might have concluded that adults cannot be trusted or are not worth the bother. The child is likely to exhibit unhealthy levels of independence, brittleness, self-assertiveness, and discomfort, especially in the presence of adults. For teachers and schools the child is also likely to be a "problem" case.

For many children, meanwhile, organized religion exerts less claim as a moral instructor than in the past. Many children grow up today as nonbelievers: The popularization of psychology, the study of primitive cultures, and the illuminating discoveries of science, all of which offer existential and universal explanations as plausible as those found in the Bible, have acted as preferred guides for their parents. Not surprisingly, many young people—along with their parents—consider earlier guides to conduct, including a Protestant-based work ethic, to be overly harsh, benighted, or repressive.

The secularizing trend of the last half-century has made the public school's task more difficult. Schools today are widely expected to instill self-discipline, and at the same time they are supposed to remain officially neutral to the moral precepts that undergirded the goal of universal schooling in the first place. These precepts drew heavily from the Calvinist ethos developed in the seventeenth century but shared to a large degree by Jesuit, rabbinical, neoclassical, and bourgeois traditions. They idealized a self-regulated life built on prudence, reserve, frugality, honesty, courage, lack of idleness, the use of liberty and talents toward productive ends, as well as the resistance of temptation so as to achieve a state of grace. In a word, discipline.

The public schools have never been—and should not try to become—centers of spiritual training. But they used to benefit from the near-universal spiritual instruction of the young in religious families and in houses of worship—and from the almost universal sense among teachers that they should organize their own and their charges' lives in accord with traditional moral precepts. Now, at least in cosmopolitan areas, the public school's faculty and clientele are likely to include fundamentalists, secularists, agnostics, and atheists. And since 1962 court interpretations of the First Amendment have been extremely sensitive to clients who resent the official presence of a Protestant-tinged educational moral system, including an old-fashioned work ethic. By common consent, especially among beleaguered school officials, the Calvinist outlook has been gradually demoted from a favored ideal to the status of one morality competing with other points of view. The merits of relativism can be debated, but a school posture that seems to make juvenile self-regulation voluntary frustrates many parents—and not only evangelicals—who fear that the school bus carries their children to places where their own values are mocked or held in low esteem. Not a few of them decide to leave their community schools for private institutions that reflect their moral bias.

If certain educative institutions—including family, neighborhood, and religion—lose the power to gain the attention of youth, other entities will gain it. No young person remains wholly untutored. For good or ill, someone or something will provide models of acceptable behavior, set standards of conduct, impart life's lore, and transmit stories of the past. If some authorities lapse, others will replace them.

The most potent source of influence on children and adolescents, beyond parents, is their circle of friends. Even when children enjoy an intimate a friendly relationship with their families, peer groups offer standards of conduct that matter intensely. Each group offers a standard of conduct that is more stable, uniform, and predictable than the standards of the community at large. And since parental views of how children should behave tend to vary widely and conflict in outlook, peer groups have gained increased power to shape the charac-

81

ter of their members and to influence relations between parents and children.

For even small children, each peer group puts forward its own version of what family life should be. It sets standards of achievement and style, determining in part what attitudes and manners should be imitated. It circulates information about what parental regulations are in force, what regulations can be violated safely, and what is the norm of parenthood. Children bonded to any particular peer group, then, convey disapproval to their own parents when the apparent norm is violated. The peer group, the historian Christopher Lasch has said, becomes an organized interest group for children. And most parents step quickly to its dictations. In defying the peer group, many believe they risk losing their own credibility or their child's devotion.

Of ascendant educating authorities, though, the strongest force is television. There is a television set in virtually every U.S. household. And "neither age, reading ability, intelligence, nor an admission fee limits access," George Comstock, a Syracuse University communications professor, points out. On the average, during a typical winter week children between two and eleven watch thirty-one hours of television, according to A. C. Nielsen researchers. For teenagers between twelve and seventeen the participation rate drops to twenty-four hours. Lower-income and minority children spend even more average time in front of the television, mainly because they have fewer alternate recreational opportunities than do other children.

Each year an average child watches about 20,000 commercials. According to numerous studies, advertising dollars are well spent. Children make numerous requests for products they learn about on television, and in the words of a recent report, experience "disappointment, anger, and conflict" when parents deny their requests.

By now television's ability to provoke consumption and antisocial acts by children is well documented. Research shows, too, that television can reduce children's attention span. It evidently stunts the academic development of heavy watchers, making them less patient with expository presentations, less able to generate their own detailed private fantasies, and less agile at translating printed symbols into thoughts. A 1980 California state assessment of sixth- and twelfth-graders found an inverse relationship between rates of television watching and performance on academic achievement tests. "The relationship was very strong, and none of several other factors—such as socioeconomic status and English language fluency—that were analyzed substantially affected it," the California report concluded.

Television also cuts at the margin between childhood and adulthood. It reveals secrets, mysteries, contradictions, and tragedies once considered inaccessible to or unsuitable for children. Television programming oscillates between feigned celebrations of traditional values and luxurious, slightly kinky images. In its treatment of children and adolescents, however, television is resolutely modern, adhering to the position that adults and young people should strive to achieve a democratic and "understanding" relationship.

Consider the implications of a recent hour-long drama. An overly strict white teacher, recovering from a nervous breakdown, is taunted unmercifully by a black student for her rigid academic standards. (The conflict is not racial. The teacher also irritates white varsity athletes who must finish their assignments in study hall before going to basketball practice.) Whether she can bear his insults and disruptions is touch-and-go for forty-five minutes. But then, after viewers are exposed to the boy's pathetic cravings for attention and respect, the student himself goes berserk and tries to murder her. Displaying remarkable courage in front of her class as she disarms him, the teacher realizes how emotionally strong she is. Her rigidity falls like scales. Afterward, gently, she visits the boy in the hospital where he is being "treated."

A touching story, yes, but also one with upsetting undertones. The teacher's rigidity seems directly linked to her past mental disorders. Thus, it is implied, teachers who are strict probably suffer from nameless hangups. The student, in spite of his felonious act, is presented as a victim and utterly absolved of guilt, possibly driven over the edge by his teacher's standards. So it seems the boy has done the teacher a service: In the last scene the audience witnesses an epiphany of self-realization, transforming a shrew into a "feeling" individual.

On television positive models of intelligent adults are rare. Intellectual quest and achievement are almost never portrayed as legitimate, much less exemplary, activities. Highly educated, erudite, or discerning television characters are invariably presented as snobbish, repressed,

83

effete, or conniving. In stories set at a school, young male teachers look highly athletic and very probably are coaches. Older men are administrators, buffoons, or pedants. Traditionalists on the faculty tend to be stick-in-the-muds, out of touch with the (more important) therapeutic concerns of their (usually younger) colleagues. Students who get high grades are suspect; they are usually goody-goodies, sycophants, or loners. Bookish boys are not virile, we may conclude, and smart girls are not pretty.

Television is a mixed blessing. It can inform or arouse, introduce children to worlds beyond their locality or undercut the qualities of patience and sustained attention on which school learning depends. Furthermore, its hyperkinetic visual imagery can reduce the appeal of the printed word. Obsessed with a satisfying resolution, television programming and commercials can also deliver facile lessons on how problems are fixed and wishes gratified, all within thirty seconds or thirty minutes.

For some young people rock music may be more deforming than any conceivable television programming. The vast preponderance of rock output is probably innocuous, but a certain genre of song makes a point of vulgarity and morbidity. Themes emphasize national corruption and despair, the joy of drugs and Dionysian sex, or blind rage against the adult world. These lyrics—and the highly publicized lifestyles of the performers who sing them—send influential, seductive dispatches to the young, intended to be hostile to pride, temperance, effort, and order.

THE ADULT WORLD IN CRISIS

As old systems of kinship, belief, and moral conduct weaken, society's elders exhibit moods of insecurity, anxiety, skepticism, and cynicism—sentiments inevitably affecting the way youths adjust to the world in which they grow up.

These depressed moods have foundation. The smug but contained Victorian world against which people of all ages still revolt has been in decline for seventy or more years. Concurrently, inflamed nineteenth-century belief in social progress has given way to an ominous sense of impending cataclysm: Two unprecedented global wars have offered up 40 million dead, and acts of genocide continue to be reported in the back pages of newspapers; socialist ideology and at least one great economic depression have undercut popular faith in the morality and efficacy of capitalism; global resources shudder at rising global expectations, acquisitiveness, and sense of material entitlement; mass tastes, especially in the democracies, tend ever more toward the showy, commercialized, and irrational. Above all looms the real possibility of nuclear annihilation. The accumulated future-fear of many adults has been well communicated to the young.

Barring possible catastrophes, there are other sources of uncertainty. No longer does the demand for labor seem capable of infinite expansion. An emerging information society may need far fewer workers than an industrial economy; foreign competition and technological refinements may render many young citizens superfluous as producers. Given the possibility that scholastic performance might not pay later rewards, some young people decide not to bother. Achievement requires hard work and drudgery, which they believe they can avoid at little or no cost. A few appear content to become wards of the welfare state.

Beset by self-doubt or despair and seeing what may be a worse world ahead for their children, many adults have become uncertain how to treat the young. Some are not sure what interpretations of the past, facts about the present, and advice for the future to give. No longer secure in their ability to direct juvenile lives to the good, some adults, especially in the college-educated and intellectual elites, have called for more egalitarian adult–child relationships, increased childhood rights, and diminished adult interventions in children's affairs.

Permissiveness harks back to the Deweyans. As early as 1961 the sociologist James S. Coleman discerned that traditional adult controls over adolescents were waning, as a "youth culture" carved out for itself a world of heretofore unimagined leisure and autonomy. But the permissive mode of childrearing today stems most from mid-sixties intergenerational discord. At that time, citing the aridity of the work ethic and the immorality of military aggression, not to mention the repressiveness of dominant social conventions, self-righteous youths shamed many elders into moral abdication. Permissiveness became a way by which adults could avoid conflict with assertive children. And some adults, seeing in youth the mythic representations of what they had found lacking in their own lives, searched for sagacity and probity among the young and pure. For a time, youth seemed to embody singularly the virtues of vitality, imagination, and creativity.

The discordant sixties have passed, leaving their legacy. Today many parents, teachers, and other adults raised during that time try reflexively to tolerate any juvenile act, no matter how obnoxious, troubling, or destructive, so as not to appear uptight, illiberal, or insensitive. Remembering the intense generational conflicts of the past, they are eager to avoid standard-setting that young people might challenge successfully. But in doing so adults in general and teachers in particular relinquish the vestiges of their moral trust to clarify and communicate their heritage and noblest values. As a result many youths are deprived of dialogue with confident, steering elders—and denied satisfactory models for their own adulthood.

CREEPING ANOMIE

Millions of students still participate in science fairs, attend 4-H and Junior Achievement conventions, and excel on the athletic field, remaining good-natured strivers. But for some others the times are hazardous. Some young people today grow up disconnected and alienated, the victims of freedom and neglect. They are an unhappy and resentful army of the young, to be found in cities, suburbs, and country—confused, jaded, self-centered, self-destructive, and potentially violent.

Some symptoms of youthful malaise require brief description.

BOREDOM

Adults working at backroad elementary schools and municipal high schools make the same observation. A growing number of students who might once have been alert and eager pupils now are likely to be contentious, sullen, and irritable. Such students make no effort to hide their distaste for school or subject matter. They challenge teachers to justify the value of any topic in the curriculum. Any difficult, abstract, or inaccessible exercise is in mortal danger of being instantly dismissed as boring and thereby unworthy of further attention. "Teachers are burning out in front of their classes every day because they can't make the Bill of Rights as gripping as the latest Rolling Stones album," says one Harvard researcher. "And the failure of schools may ultimately stem from a simple fact. Teachers can't and shouldn't try."

Boredom is an ancient affliction, of course. But prior to our own day, at least for the masses, a struggle for existence precluded such a sentiment. Any child not engaged in serious study worked as a manual laborer or apprentice, going to work at what we now consider a cruelly young age. Today, the tables have turned. Everyone knows the ill effects that result from a child's working too hard. What is less well understood is what happens when a child's energy economy is violated in the direction of too little work. Very possibly, as the education scholar Paul Copperman has pointed out, the individual becomes self-destructive or socially destructive. For today's children, arguably, the combination of unprecedented leisure, inadequate challenges, and passive entertainment gives rise to confusion, lethargy, and self-indulgence. In quest of palliatives for monotony, thrill-seeking proceeds. Advanced boredom includes what the sociologist Robert Nisbet calls "the unmistakable if not always fully voiced longing for some kind of secular redeemer," the millenarian outlook that replaces "faith, belief, or interest in progress." In other words, salvation appears in the form of the radiant individual who may be the latest rock group or television superstar, if not the Reverend Moon.

CYNICISM

Some cunning youngsters, well aware of the pitfalls of inactivity, turn inward to advance their own self-interests. They are the new social Darwinists. But unlike former enthusiasts of unbridled competition,

87

they do not see themselves as players in an ordained, deterministic, and ultimately benign system. They are contemptuous of what they believe to be an immoral and tainted society; they consider themselves successful if they can at once control and condemn it. They are skilled at evading or undercutting sedulous adult authority. By allying themselves to libertarian rhetoric and manipulating indulgent adults, they are effective at neutralizing (even embarrassing) unyielding authority figures. In schools they base their actions in the language of personal entitlements and rights; many are well versed in the limits on the powers of their educators. These students demand good grades for little achievement; in matters of discipline or possible failure, they always want another chance. When school personnel are not accommodating to individual wants, their aggressive challenges often lead to disruptions centered on alleged adult insensitivity.

Cynical youngsters, Lasch and others have argued, have difficulty forming authentic reciprocal relationships, developing the capacity for empathy, or putting others before themselves. But when many educators are uncomfortable with standard-setting, are eager to be popular with their students, are afraid of losing face by imposing unenforceable sanctions, or are hamstrung by the specter of lawsuits, such students often triumph (at their own expense) over institutional norms and requirements. In frustrating school controls, they also serve notice to more conscientious youth that deference, diligence, and honesty may be the policy of fools.

Despair

Far more pitiful are young people who hold extremely pessimistic views about the present and future. When the best promise is a dreary job and global self-destruction may be imminent, they say, striving is pointless. Often such students feel entirely isolated from adults and have no sense of rooted values. If they have a circle of friends, it may be the single communal association to be regarded as protective and reliable. Not infrequently, such peer groups are bound by the glue of resentment and the urge for retribution. School may be perceived as a shared prison. Among such young people family problems are often advanced and intractable. Among these unfortunates a morbid spirit of *carpe diem* may punctuate a chronic state of depression and hopelessness.

DRUG ABUSE

Youngsters—including teenagers—are immature and vulnerable, without the intellectual and emotional resources of their elders. When robbed of their innocence or hope at an early age, they are apt to seek temporary oblivion.

In many middle and secondary schools today drugs are generally treated as an uncontrollable, ubiquitous fact of student life. Most parents and educators are simply resigned to these intoxicants; others, who consider themselves young at heart, wink at or condone them. If alcohol is also classified as a "problem substance," levels of adolescent drug abuse become plaguelike in intensity. This drug use suggests widespread juvenile effort to relieve boredom and loneliness chemically.

Reliable data on drug habits provide another unsettling index of modern childhood's special perils. Between 1970 and 1978 marijuana use by children eighteen or younger soared and then leveled off at very high levels. Cocaine and amphetamine use is still on the rise. In 1981 about 50 percent of high school seniors admitted that they had used marijuana in the last year. About one in ten smoked it daily. Rates tended to be higher in metropolitan—including suburban—areas. About 29 percent of eighth- and ninth-graders reported having tried it. The figure stood at 8 percent for sixth- and seventh-graders.

Heavy marijuana users tend to experiment with and abuse other drugs, such as cocaine, hallucinogens, amphetamines, sedatives, and, occasionally, heroin. And *all* public junior high and high school students have at least peripheral contact with drugs and drug users, even if they abhor drugs themselves. There is enormous peer pressure to experiment with marijuana. Almost no secondary-level student has difficulty obtaining it. He or she typically purchases it on or near campus, experiences little or no guilt about using it, and has no fear of being arrested.

To what effect? Marijuana, the least noxious of drugs, forces most pediatric authorities to equivocate. If adolescents use marijuana for entertainment instead of escape, if they are relatively mature and emotionally stable, if they are goal-oriented, if they have close ties with adults, if they use marijuana moderately and in company, then marijuana may be classified as a recreational, euphoric drug. But for youth who begin using marijuana early or frequently, these *ifs* are probably not operative. For them, marijuana—whose effects may be aggravated by other drugs—seems to *retard* ego formation, *corrode* goal-orientation, and *loosen* ties with adults. Heavy marijuana use may also impair reading comprehension, speech, long-term memory storage, quick judgment, and other mental skills.

For those students who affiliate themselves with a peer group where drug-taking is a principal source of fellowship, associations with the "straight" world diminish. As any perceptive teacher who has watched a tenth-grader on a chemical treadmill can attest, tragic personality changes occur. "At school, surreptitious existence is all-consuming, like that of John LeCarré characters operating behind enemy lines," one Washington-based specialist says. "These kids are suspicious of adults, always vigilant, contemptuous of outsiders, and eager to flaunt their life-style during recess or in the school bus, advertising to other kids how fun it is to be high all day."

Experts agree that alcohol, too, has become an early and often indispensable element of teenage social life. This would be a less disturbing fact if juvenile drinking were in fact confined to the proverbial "beer or two with the boys." But to many teenagers, even on a school night, "let's party" means something different. A recent survey reports that one out of sixteen high school students drinks on a *daily* basis. The combination of alcohol and automobiles, which too often translates into reckless adolescent driving, accounts for heavy carnage for teenagers and others, especially in suburban and rural communities. Yet, if a child passes out after drinking half a bottle of Bacardi, even weekly, some parents will avert their eyes—comforted, at least, that their fifteen-year-old has no taste for hallucinogens.

CASUAL SEX

When does a teenager's sexuality become self-destructive? No one is certain, even as sexual intercourse among high school students becomes ordinary and expected. During the last decade, among the various teenage cohorts, the rate of sexual intercourse has risen most rapidly—doubled—for white youth between the ages of fourteen and sixteen. According to a 1979 Johns Hopkins survey, about 70 percent of unmarried girls aged fifteen to nineteen living in metropolitan areas are, to use the conventional phrase, "sexually active." In spite of sex education and well-publicized contraceptive techniques, one out of three fourteen-year-old girls today faces the prospect of having an abortion or giving birth to an illegitimate child before the age of nineteen.

Only to the terminally dissolute can these trends suggest wholesome sexual liberation and nothing more. Teenage sex may no longer give one a "reputation." The "bad girl" of the past is now virtually extinct. But as the old ideal of chastity has lost its authority, new troubles have surfaced: fierce peer pressure for some boys and girls to engage in sexual intercourse at a very young age; coping with the emotional effects of intimacy; promiscuity; declining respect for sexual involvement; and often, trauma for those who indulge as children, presumably trying to capture the intimacy and affection that elude them in other areas of their lives.

DELINQUENCY

In middle-class communities student "white-collar" crime exists: cheating, drug-dealing, and vandalism, all at incalculable levels. Only occasionally does a lurid event permit us to glimpse the world of alienated suburban teenagers before it fades swiftly from the news.*

* One thinks of a 1981 Milpitas, California, murder of a fourteen-year-old girl by her boyfriend. Many classmates inspected her half-nude body that lay for days in the hills above the town. One poked the corpse with sticks; another ripped a decal advertising a local radio station off her discarded jeans. In spite of rumors flying around the high school campus, no student reported the incident to any adult for days. "You don't narc [inform] on people," said one friend of the victim by way of explanation.

91

In half-abandoned urban neighborhoods from Anacostia to Compton, where poverty adds to despair, childhood anomie takes a different turn. Here, some fourth- and fifth-graders are already street-wise, experienced hands at taking care of themselves and younger siblings in an unheated February apartment without mother or father, at hustling the social worker and the general hospital, at mingling with the older men who let them drink beer out of paper bags. A rudimentary sense of compassion or social contract escapes them. They dream of someday being Superfly or The Man. They are typically black- or brown-skinned. Not only are they completely alienated from school; the schools are afraid of them.

By the age of ten or twelve some of these youngsters have become incorrigible truants. They have learned that crime pays. Their exploits, from purse-snatching to arson, are well known. What few people realize, however, is that metropolitan police now concede they are losing control over these delinquents. Consider the highly respected New York City Police Commissioner Robert J. McGuire's words to *The New York Times:*

> Sometimes I ask myself, 'Are we being hysterical? Wasn't there crime before? Are we getting old and old-fashioned?' No. This isn't the same. The statistics are three, four, five times what they were 20 years ago. And the pathology is much worse. The kids who prey on people have a look in their eyes that says 'your life isn't worth anything to me.' Whether they injure you is irrelevant to them. Random. Gratuitous. Like pulling wings off butterflies, only the butterflies are people. . . . If the social contract is breaking apart, then all the police can do is conduct a holding action. Everything always works its way back to the things people don't want to talk about—morality, application of values, anything other than their obsession with instant gratification.

THE QUESTION OF PERMISSIVENESS

It is said that children are freer, have more rights, and grow up earlier than at any time in the past. What is said less often is that more children than at any time in memory are also unhappy, feckless, and adrift. Who is so hard-hearted as to ignore this accumulating suffering and wreckage? Who can be so brazen as to say that the changing world of childhood reflects unalloyed social progress?

Schools cannot mend families or eradicate the Gong Show. They cannot compete with video games or triple-X-rated films. But conscious that other social compasses now spin out of control, schools can at least try to stand for moral and intellectual fixity. In educational theory and elsewhere the values of toleration and individualism have been well advertised. But at the cost of norms: At the extremes, all is permitted and justifiable, nothing is necessary or impossible.

Educators and others who resent norms for children and themselves should consider the danger to liberty. The freedom so beloved by First and Fourteenth Amendment activists does not come without a cost. Civil liberties require public compromise: Democratic society cannot stand to act as a mere collection of individuals, each member defining public values as he or she sees fit, forcibly committed to nothing beyond self. The habit of compromise is lost. People forget their talents at living moderately, between Chaos and Leviathan.

As social agencies in a democracy, public schools have a moral trust to act as stabilizing forces. To do this effectively they seem to be required to offer what the philosopher R. S. Peters calls a provisional morality, an ethical code that individuals must accept as children but can question as adults. Effective learning environments require, first, self-control, respect for adults, and love of work on the part of young people. Modish adults who remain hostile or neutral to such primary values do the schools and children no good.

SIX

The Common School
in Crisis

IN THE NAME OF EQUALITY ABOVE ALL, the common-school ideal
has become the servant of two masters. On one hand it is supposed
to honor the conflicting claims of fractious school constituencies, all
with competing dispositions toward schooling and views of childrearing. On the other, it has a public charge to mix and educate (in harmony) youth of every class, race, capability, and outlook. This dual
aspect of the public school—at once trying to accommodate differences
and guarantee sameness—has become extreme and contradictory, grandiose in conception and impossible to execute. Arguably, the common-
school ideal in its current guise impedes the quest for scholastic quality,
inducing increased educational polarities and preventing the establishment of universal standards of excellence.

For well over a century extending the reach of formal education
to all has been the first principle of U.S. school reform. But reformers
have grown steadily more ambitious and utopian. In 1900 the common-
school ideal meant that primary schools should provide, at public
expense, universal access to the fundamentals of language and arithmetic, along with heavy doses of Protestant ethics. By 1950 it went only

94

so far as to mean that districts should build "comprehensive" public high schools available to every adolescent (nonetheless, retaining awesome power to track pupils according to ability). Even then, only about 55 percent of young people remained in school long enough to earn a high school diploma, and of course most black youth were segregated in scandalously inferior schools. During the last generation this old democratizing ideal has been much elaborated, sometimes with salutary effects for minority and handicapped students. Yet by trying to secure ever more pure common schools, recent reformers have advocated measures that have placed many public systems in jeopardy.

When idealism loses touch with human imperfections, it often becomes unreasonable. When public policy is based on wishful thinking, it usually tends toward self-righteous and doomed initiatives. And when initiatives turn into crusades, reformers become less interested in *what works* and more interested in *loyalty to the cause.* Time and again, as a result, social reform movements have been derailed. Diverse equity drives in education, now blatantly favoring special groups and antimeritocratic values, are no exception. Today in America's schools, there is no more shocking an inequality than in the spectrum of institutional academic and behavioral standards.

During the last few years a number of disturbing turns in school demography and finance have become evident. But these grim signs have been largely ignored, misinterpreted, or suppressed, mainly because they highlight disagreeable issues of socioeconomic class and race. Yet before authentic school reform can take place, school observers must acknowledge some noxious trends and tendencies that liberal reformers could not foresee in the sixties and seventies.

First, recent extensions of the common-school ideal have not generally yielded better schools in terms of cognition and character. Second, attempts to diversify student bodies by decree and against community have often backfired, especially when large lower-class populations have been placed suddenly in middle-class schools and when middle-class parents have had easy access to suburban or private alternatives. Third, and in part as a consequence, metropolitan housing patterns and school districts have come to correspond more and more sharply to class and race. Because of this, James S. Coleman warns, "the common-school ideal [as currently conceived in terms of ethnic mixture] may no longer be attainable through *any* means, short of highly coercive ones." Fourth, middle-class taxpayers have become less and less interested in financing public schools, particularly those swollen with nonacademic responsibilities for lower-class children.

It is time to face some facts. From schools and districts where indifference to learning is rampant and pastoral concerns seem to prevail, middle-class parents who hold high ambitions for their children will over time withdraw their support and patronage. The working class and coping poor—on whom new common-school initiatives are most likely to fall directly—may try to do the same in spite of crushing financial obstacles. What is called white flight is actually interracial middle-class flight, seeming racial in character only because so many more minority than white families are trapped in the lower class. Middle-class flight's first cause is not racial antipathy but middle-class alarm at the standards in force at schools where most pupils come from disadvantaged backgrounds. Also, the apparent absence of serious scholastic standards in predominantly lower-class schools sends the signal to many taxpayers that minority students are incapable of meeting such standards. It is hard to imagine a more insidious spur to resurgent racial prejudice.

As long as inferior educational standards persist in schools for the lower class, most minority students will remain isolated from full educational access and opportunity. This form of inequality will have divisive and deleterious impact on the culture: The middle class of all races will seek superior educational alternatives for its children, if need be in the private sector, and pay less and less attention to the common-school ideal. Private schools will continue to thrive, as some school experts say they should. For as we shall see, in some localities today nonpublic schools provide about the only chance a lower-class child has to experience the kind of schooling that many middle-class children take for granted.

In many localities the most basic reversal during the last thirty years has been *desegregation by race* and *resegregation by class.* The exception to this rule is to be found in the rural Southeast. Ironically, in Southern agricultural communities today one finds the most thoroughgoing and successful racial integration anywhere in the country. Common elementary and secondary schools have replaced dual school systems. The children of local physicians, commodities warehousemen, electricians, and tenant farmers attend school together without much friction. These common-schools-by-decree have succeeded on account of special circumstances, notably: the relentless activity of federal officials in the sixties and seventies to blot out vestiges of de jure segregation, the injection of federal money to improve local education plants, the unlikelihood or impossibility of white flight from newly integrated schools, *and* the consensual social values held by middle-class and lower-class families because of near-universal protestant religious training.

Take, for example, one typical Southern high school, 70 percent white and 30 percent black, located in a North Carolina tobacco town with a population of 3,600. Here, as may be the rule at any school, students tend to select companions of similar family background, levels of intelligence, and out-of-school interests. They are also conscious of racial differences. In the lunchroom and on campus, blacks and whites segregate themselves voluntarily. After school white students tend to hang out next to their cars, which few black students own. The school handbook requires students to select a Prom Queen and Homecoming Queen of different colors. But it would be hard to find a more harmonious and pacific secondary school anywhere in the country. It is difficult to believe that, until twelve years ago, blacks and whites in this town were schooled entirely apart.

For black and white students equally, though, this is an academically substandard school. Most students are tracked early on into threadbare vocational programs. The school has no proper American history course, and not until the eleventh grade does the regular English course introduce students to what is called the five-paragraph essay. Eighteen percent of the student body, blacks and whites at about the same rate, failed the state competency test in basic skills the first year it was given. In this town racial integration has presumably increased educational opportunities for black if not white children. While it has not impelled high scholastic outcomes, neither has it been an impediment to learning. Meanwhile, local citizens have come to accept a healthy and overdue social mixture.

But what has been a limited good for the rural Southeast has not worked in most metropolitan areas. Historically, public schools were organized by residential districts (rather than by an individual student's social class or tested intelligence). Until mid-century district organization tended to create common schools, for community schools attracted a broad (but toward the end of high school, not a full) cross-section of a locality. And in districts outside the segregated South where nonwhite enrollments were minuscule, the issue of racial mixture in schools simply never came up. Since the fifties, however, many middle- and working-class whites, seeking improved residential amenities, have moved to more economically stratified and racially distinct suburban districts.

Simultaneously, millions of poor blacks and Hispanics have migrated from rural areas of the U.S. South, from Mexico, and from the Caribbean to concentrate in Northern and Western cities. Their children have become a large cohort—during the last decade a majority—in many urban districts (Table 6–1). Above all, urban schools have faced increasing numbers of lower-class students who have trouble learning. When frustrated or alienated, these pupils frequently disrupt classrooms, make schoolyards unsafe, and flamboyantly ignore middle-class educational values. Not unexpectedly, downtown districts have tried to accommodate these unhappy newcomers, gradually adapting to negative attitudes toward schooling. Many city educators, accustomed to home climates unsupportive of academic achievement, have introduced numerous schoolhouse social services to make up for parental inability or negligence, have taken ambivalent postures toward the value of "white culture," and have tolerated student behavior that middle-class parents find offensive or immoral.

In many cities, as a result, the middle class has ascertained correctly that it no longer controls the municipal school system. Many white families feel, perhaps incorrectly, that their children are welcome in city schools only as racial-balancing factors. Some believe that many urban school personnel resent their children or are less than interested in meeting the academic needs of eager pupils. In central cities middle-class parents typically learn through the grapevine which district-

98

TABLE 6–1
School Enrollment in 10 U.S. Cities by Ethnic Group, 1970 and 1980
(in Order of 1980 Enrollment Size)

The number of students, in thousands, is in parentheses, and enrollment proportions are given to the nearest whole percentage. An asterisk denotes less than 0.6 percent.

	WHITE	BLACK	HISPANIC	ASIAN
New York City				
1970 (1,141)	38	34	26	2
1980 (944)	28	38	30	3
Los Angeles				
1970 (643)	50	24	22	4
1980 (538)	24	23	45	7
Chicago				
1970 (578)	35	54	10	1
1980 (445)	19	60	19	2
Dade County (Miami)				
1970 (240)	54	25	21	*
1980 (233)	32	30	38	*
Philadelphia				
1970 (280)	36	61	3	*
1980 (224)	29	63	7	1
Detroit				
1970 (274)	35	64	1	*
1980 (211)	12	86	2	*
Dallas				
1970 (164)	57	34	9	*
1980 (130)	30	50	19	1
Washington, D.C.				
1970 (145)	5	95	*	*
1980 (100)	4	95	1	*
Atlanta				
1970 (109)	31	68	*	*
1980 (72)	8	91	*	*
Boston				
1970 (97)	64	30	4	2
1980 (67)	35	46	14	5
Nation at large				
1970 (44,900)	79	15	5	*
1980 (39,400)	73	16	8	2

Source: Derived from data collected by the Council of Great City Schools, Washington, D.C.

schools do and do not stress achievement, standard English speech patterns, high student ambitions, and courteous manners. If such school options are unattainable, the grim educational situation may provide the final impetus for them to leave the district, thus intensifying its lower-class character.*

Once in the suburban ring, purchasing a house and making mortgage payments, middle-class families, consciously or unconsciously, pay hidden tuition—and receive a hidden federal tax subsidy in the form of property tax writeoffs—for schools they believe capable of realizing their children's potential. "The most exclusive schools in America are suburban *public* schools," the education finance scholar Thomas Vitullo-Martin has concluded. "Enrollment in them is determined by stringent economic criteria, by the family's having enough capital to buy a house in a high income school district." Adds Coleman: "The residential basis of school assignment, in an ironic twist, has proved to be segregative and exclusionary."

Meanwhile, suburban white taxpayers perceive in city schools the crucible of a welfare-dependent underclass, expanding, delinquent, unemployable, full of emnity, and seemingly immune to education. They sense that prevailing racial policies and sentiments in urban education may sabotage their own values by scorning blacks who embrace and emulate bourgeois habits as "oreos," black on the outside but white within. They wonder if bad city schools are helping to create demoralized and undeserving poor people.

While taxpayers grow more disgruntled, the wing of the education establishment in charge of its racial policies and sentiments still seems unwilling to police itself and those it professes to assist. Those who preside over urban and minority education through their control of payrolls, their power to draft equal opportunity legislation, and their ability to direct civil rights litigation also determine the official lines of liberal reasoning on this subject. And according to prevalent think-

* Between 1970 and 1980 white enrollments dropped by 82 percent in Atlanta, 74 percent in Detroit, 62 percent in Boston, and 60 percent in Los Angeles. Nonwhite enrollments are not always evenly proportioned by grade: in Los Angeles in 1982, the twelfth grade was 30 percent Hispanic, the kindergarten 62 percent. Part of white shrinkage can be explained by the declining national birthrate. But in most major cities the decline in white enrollments during the decade was more than double the 19 percent drop in white enrollments nationally.

ing among them, a view more often implied than badly stated, non-whites should not have to meet the same performance standards in schools as whites. When minorities fail or do not advance, it is said, white racism, elitism, ethnocentrism, and exclusionism are at fault. When minorities have difficulty meeting a standard, the reflex is to lower, abolish, or blur the standard, or to substitute another. In setting educational policies, these authorities have trafficked in political images more than in results, have demanded preferential treatment for their constituents, and have misused white compassion. They have refused to exhort minority youth to higher levels of initiative, achievement, and morality. They appear willing even now to maintain low-income minorities as perpetual claimants, dependent on transfer payments, innocent of the notion of self-help.

This situation cannot abide forever. The operation of urban schools ultimately depends on taxpayer generosity. And not only are middle-class citizens taking a distant and stingy attitude toward urban schools. The number of taxpayers with a personal stake in *any* school improvement is diminishing. During the last ten years the portion of U.S. adults with school-age children has fallen from 41 to 28 percent. An aging electorate is already voicing its preference for other social services, such as police protection, social security, health care, and public transportation. Public schools, then, face significant community groups not eager to increase school budgets, including older adults whose own children have finished school; younger adults who are buying high-quality schools through property or tuition payments; younger adults and aging taxpayers who are unmarried or who have no children; and working-class parents, especially in rural areas, who are satisfied with substandard schools because they attended similar schools.

Where will the money come from? Champions of special-interest school programs and parents who rely on schools to provide extra services for their children have for years leaned on the federal treasury. As it permits states and localities to fund new programs painlessly, Washington's money has been much appreciated. But no matter who controls Congress or the White House in coming years, those accustomed or addicted to federal handouts are likely to be disappointed: Structural strains on the federal budget (e.g., a saturated national

101

deficit, the absence of low-cost energy, the demands of the Pentagon) make it almost certain that states and localities will soon assume greater responsibilities for general and categorical education costs. The question, then, is unavoidable: In coming years, how willing will taxpayers be to fund public schools, especially those they find so objectionable that they refuse to patronize them?

⌣

Increased interest in private schooling is a central educational issue of our times. At its most obvious it reflects a middle- and working-class vote of no confidence in heralded school reforms. But the willingness to look elsewhere, beyond the public system, has deeper social implications. "It is the line between the private and public that represents the most radical division in the character of American education," Syracuse University's education professor Gerald Grant comments. "The great paradox in American education today is that only the privates have a public in the classical sense." By 1983 private school enrollments had reached about 5 million or roughly 11 percent of all school enrollments. And the robust condition of nonpublic schools was inextricably linked to wider displeasure over public school policies and outcomes, to the sense that many public schools had been politicized in line with left-wing social doctrine, and to cooling enthusiasm and support for the common-school ideal.

To most educational leaders, though, the rising interest in private schools was nothing more than an unjust, undemocratic, and vaguely sinister trend to be stamped out by the forces of light. An American Enterprise Institute policy analyst, Denis P. Doyle, describes the official stereotype:

> The voluntarism [that private schools] represent is viewed as escapist and exclusive, rather than communitarian and normative. Independent day and boarding schools are viewed as the bastions of privilege and elitism, high-tuition schools that enroll the children of the nation's power elites. Traditional parochial schools, principally Catholic and Lutheran, enroll not the elites of commerce and academe, but the shock troops of the working class, the "hard hats" of urban America. And Christian Academies are the special

102

province of the evangelical red-neck, who, as he praises the Lord, condemns the blacks, and retreats to a white-flight academy.

Such imagery was graphic and politically convenient, said Doyle. It was also wildly simplistic. The new private school clientele included others than the rich and the Roman Catholic: At old-line schools it included the children of middle-level professionals and executives upset by large, listless, undemanding suburban schools; at urban parochial schools it included the children of the aspiring poor, including large numbers of non-Catholics; at Christian schools it included the children of evangelicals and fundamentalists who felt more morally than racially displaced from the public schools. Most of this clientele wanted the public schools to be good, and many parents remembered their own public schooling with affection and pride. Such families were leaving the public sector hesitantly, having reached the undesired conclusion that their local public schools might not be good for their children's mind or heart.

And how did these families pay? Some, deciding to raise a small number of children, had considerable disposable income per child, hence extra money for tuition. But most families, even those with executive-level incomes, had to sacrifice. In every case they sacrificed to provide their children with educational environments that they felt were high in quality and operated in accord with their individual tastes.

During the early eighties, private school enrollments expanded most rapidly for so-called Christian academies. Today, at least 7,000 such schools, usually of small size, operate in church basements, defunct motels, leased public school buildings, and on other *ad hoc* sites. From the kindergarten to the senior high level, they school some 1 million pupils. These school communities are bound by faith in basic skills, school prayer, creationism, puritanic values, and unabashed patriotism. They reject explicitly the notion that schools should tolerate a wide variety of outlooks and that schooling should be separated from religion.

The impulse behind Christian schools, and a forceful one, is to separate children from ethical climates where young people are urged to reach their own conclusions as free-willed individuals. Parents in

103

fundamentalist congregations seek to sequester their young in sheltered, devout, unworldly, and essentially homogeneous educational settings where their values are not derided and where they can leave behind the losing fight against Darwin or blasphemous textbooks. In these enclaves teenage temperance and chastity are not represented as something quaint, less than ordinary, or "one point of view." Salvation, not intellectual advancement, is the ultimate aim of schooling.*

Very different has been the case of the Catholic schools, significant for their provision of superior educational services to disadvantaged students. In the early eighties the near-vertical plunge of parochial enrollments—about 40 percent between 1966 and 1976—leveled off and in many urban areas reversed itself. In the process many municipal Catholic schools expanded their business of educating minority students. Nationally, in 1982 about one-fifth of Catholic enrollments at the primary level and one-sixth at the secondary level were black or Hispanic. A National Catholic Education Association–sponsored survey in 1980 reviewed sixty-five randomly selected parochial elementary schools in downtown Chicago, Detroit, Los Angeles, Milwaukee, New Orleans, New York, and Washington, D.C. On the average the student composition was 70 percent black, Hispanic, or Asian. One-third of the students were not Catholic. Almost three-quarters of them came from families with annual incomes below $15,000 and 35 percent from families earning less than $10,000. Sixty percent of students, significantly, lived in two-parent households.

These urban parochial schools were spare operations, with clean but dilapidated buildings, underpaid teachers, and equipment in short supply. In 1982 tuition averaged $500 at the elementary level and $1,200 at the secondary level. These fees did not cover basic costs,

---

* Early on, liberals pounced on Christian schools as racially motivated "schools that fear built." In fact, the Christian school movement of the eighties, unlike the secular segregation academy movement of the sixties and early seventies, had much more to do with doctrine than with race. The "liberal" view did not account for the proliferation of Christian schools in all-white regions of the country or the presence of minority students in many Christian schools. In some cases, it is true, the establishment of evangelical schools was racially motivated, especially when school desegregation fomented interracial turmoil. But generally Christian schools resulted from fundamentalist distress over public schools that seemed to stand for alien moral values and atheism.

and reserve church funds to subsidize even bare-bones schools were dwindling. As fewer young adults chose vocations inside the church, the number of nominally paid teachers drawn from ecclesiastical ranks was falling. Increasingly, to stay in business, Catholic schools were turning to private philanthrophy and mounting ambitious development drives. Sometimes they charged higher fees to students from outside the parish.

Catholic schools received a boost in 1981, when a National Center for Education Statistics report came out, published in preliminary form over the authoritative signature of James S. Coleman. The study of private and public school quality was one early analysis of data collected by The National Opinion Research Center (commissioned by the NCES), a sample of more than 58,000 students in about 1,000 schools across the country. To the surprise of few, it concluded that private schools on the whole outperformed public schools. To the surprise of many, however, the report that was quickly dubbed "Coleman II" indicated something else: that even after adjustments for family background were made in the sample, private schools produced higher average cognitive outcomes, gave students greater self-esteem and sense of control over their fates, and were more likely to produce graduates of good character. The main reason was higher nonpublic standards. And stunningly, Coleman II concluded that better than public schools, parochial schools "approximate the 'common school' ideal . . . in that the achievement levels of students from different parental educational backgrounds, of black and Hispanic students, and of Hispanic and non-Hispanic white students are more nearly alike in Catholic schools than in public schools."

Most education commentators and public school advocates fizzled with outrage, seeing in the report a frontal assault on the public system. Facing emotional and often *ad hominem* attacks, Coleman later conceded that drawing an explicit dichotomy between effective and ineffective schools would have been a more valuable research venture. He denied that private education was inherently superior to public education. But Coleman did not pull back from his contention that poor children were being served better by the educational policies in force in private schools. "Since we know that there are school factors that make a difference," Coleman told *The New York Times,* "we might

look for ways to make public schools more like the private ones."
These were words that educational leaders could ignore only at great
risk. And a brief excursion to an unusual place explains why.

⌣⌢

On High Street, overlooking the rotted downtown of Newark, New
Jersey, stand two secondary schools, one private and one public. St.
Benedict's, a complex of red brick school buildings surrounding a
115-year-old monastery, and Central High School, built in 1913, serve
essentially the same black and Hispanic, welfare-dependent families,
who live in nearby high-rise public housing projects. St. Benedict's
produces exceptional outcomes, breaking for many of its students the
vicious cycle of poverty into which they were born. Central High is,
by contrast, typical of the least effective high schools operating in
any major city. Admittedly, St. Benedict's is more innovative than
most parochial schools. Admittedly, too, Central High encounters a
greater array of student problems than most municipal schools. A
comparison of each school's outcome must acknowledge St. Benedict's
inherent advantages: More of its students come from working families,
its clients are self-selecting, and its parents are aware of what is needed
educationally for their children to advance in station. Still, the two
schools' populations are not so different in background that comparisons are specious or meaningless.

St. Benedict's is not a fancy school. Its physical plant is clean,
if rundown. The maintenance budget is overtaxed. The 350 seventh-
through twelfth-grade boys who attend the school are selected for
motivation and ability, but few of them are gifted. Most students
pay a large or full portion of St. Benedict's $1,250 tuition, many by
working during the summer. *All* seniors take the SAT. (Median scores
in 1982 were 350 Verbal and 380 Math, well below the national average
and reflecting the student body's uneven capabilities. Individual scores
ranged from about 200 to 600 in both areas.) In 1982 the colleges
to which St. Benedict's sent its graduates included Swarthmore, Dart-
mouth, Rutgers, and Holy Cross. Other graduating seniors entered
community colleges, became apprentices in skilled trades, or went
into the armed forces.

The hub of St. Benedict's is Newark Abbey, separated from the school only by heavy oak double doors. The monastery is a pleasant place, full of dark nineteenth-century wood moldings, overstuffed chairs, stained glass, and murals depicting the glories of Christianity. On the roof of one class building the monks keep four working beehives, and bees are the school's symbol. Assisting the monks is the authoritative tradition of the 1,500-year-old Benedictine order, which, the fathers will tell anyone, has survived in and adapted to centuries as uncertain as the present.

How to trigger and sustain the motivation of minority students is the faculty's primary concern. "Many talented black kids make a point of avoiding thought," says Father Edwin, the blunt and charismatic principal. "They have played the jive role so long that their minds have atrophied." Over the last eight years the Benedictine fathers have altered their attitudes toward black students. "We used to be more accepting," says one. "We felt sorry for our students, so we didn't expect very much from them." Now the faculty is more firm. "A kid will come in and tell me he's deprived," says Father Edwin. "I'll say back, 'You haven't seen your father for ten years. You can stay paralyzed if you want or you can face facts.' Ten years ago, I would have been crying along with the kid."

Above all, the school insists on good manners and restrained behavior. Noise and rowdiness are not tolerated. Even during the passing period, when any school corridor erupts in confusion, the halls feel safe. Students do not shove one another or jostle adults. Nowhere in the school is there any trace of graffiti. St. Benedict's atmosphere is calm and energetic.

Academic demands are high. In one class, an eleventh grader reads from *Gulliver's Travels* while Father Philip shows how a Houyhnhnm might walk. Down the hall, Jack Dalton, a lay history teacher and basketball coach, walks around class in a gray tweed jacket. Suddenly he stops and asks one student why he doesn't know a word from last night's assignment. "You must learn to use a dictionary," he cautions. "You must try to fall in love with words to appreciate their many shades of meaning." Upstairs, Father Edwin's voice filters from biology class into the corridor. "Okay, those are the different kinds of compound leaves," he says. "Does everybody understand?"

Sturdy moral principles, evident in school codes and organization,

107

are reinforced in the classroom. Every student (most of the black pupils are Baptists) takes a four-year sequence of religion. Eleventh graders, for instance, learn ethics from Father Luke. In a soft, patient voice, he explains the meaning of *conscience*. To a roomful of students, who display an ordinary range of teenage classroom moods, he analyzes the word crisply and intelligently. "There is more to any issue than the law," he concludes. Later in the year Father Luke will give this section inspiriting classes in courage, honesty, and prudence.

From September to April St. Benedict's runs a rugged but conventional academic regimen. To graduate, a student must take four years each of English, social studies, religion, and physical education. The school also requires three years of mathematics (including computer science) and one year of laboratory science. Electives include Latin and economics. Classes average twenty students in size. But technically the school operates eleven months each year, beginning in July with a mandatory six-week summer school of remedial and enrichment courses. "It keeps students busy during the summer months, when they need to keep up academically, and when most of them don't have anything worthwhile to do," explains Father Edwin.

For eighty freshmen the summer session is especially taxing. Every ninth-grader is required to arrive at St. Benedict's with a sleeping bag on the first day for a live-in introduction to the school. This week-long initiation goes from 6:30 A.M. to 10:30 P.M. each day. Students are forbidden to telephone their parents. Meanwhile, they are drilled in school history and traditions and are required to write essays on what they hope to achieve in the future, do calisthenics, and serve each other meals. These exercises disarm suspicious or undisciplined youngsters, forcing them to participate immediately in the group spirit of the school. By the third day students typically have learned the names of all their classmates.

Freshmen continue to observe special rituals through the year, such as carrying a notebook at all times and walking on the proper side of the hall. Then, in May, while upperclassmen spend five weeks off-campus doing projects such as children's theater and urban field studies, they take a 42-mile backpacking trip along the entire New Jersey section of the Appalachian Trail. For three weeks, through physical exercise, map-reading assignments, and short walks, the freshmen prepare for the outing. The trip itself takes one week. There is, interestingly, a close correlation between those who fail the trip and those who ultimately fail in their studies. The emphasis on building character through fraternal striving may explain why coeducation is not a pressing matter to the faculty or students.

Strenuous athletic and extracurricular activity is encouraged. "Someone who has difficulty with math or reading can try to get by keeping quiet," Father Edwin told a congressional subcommittee on education in 1980. "On a track, on a court, a wrestling mat, or a stage, there's no place to hide. The demands are rapid, intense, clear, and the results are in right away."

Nonacademic life at the school revolves around the so-called Group System, which affords every student ample attention and at the same time a voice in school operations. The student body is divided into fourteen cooperatives, each named for an illustrious teacher or alumnus. A month after school begins, group leaders meet in strict secrecy. Using a draft system, with last year's least successful group having first choice, they pick all boys of the freshman class. From then on, in a decentralized setting, the student group and two faculty advisers work together daily, paying special attention to those members who are struggling. Most discipline is left to the group leaders, who meet regularly with the headmaster. In addition the groups compete with one another, getting points for academic excellence, high attendance rates, athletic achievement, and school service.

The central point here is not St. Benedict's "privateness" or even its somewhat irregular program. More, even a cursory description of the school makes it clear that St. Benedict's is by any measure an effective school, effective because it has the freedom to establish and enforce what a scholarly and sincere faculty believe to be exemplary standards, procedures, and customs. Any parent or child who enters St. Benedict's is expected to abide within reason by its stated standards—and thereby willingly cede some individual power. (Significantly, the threat of expulsion, though it is rarely acted on, gives St. Benedict's a means of controlling those who flagrantly disrespect those standards.) Through all of this St. Benedict's has the authority to make itself a superior school, which is not the fortune of its neighborhood competitor.

Several blocks from St. Benedict's 1,200 other students attend
Central High School. The student body—less integrated than St. Benedict's—is 98 percent black and Hispanic. Truancy rates average 26
percent daily, and class-cutting is epidemic. Consequently, individual
class meetings rarely draw much more than half of the students enrolled
in each course. Through elaborate security precautions, such as the
use of student identification tags, the disorder—one faculty member
called it "anarchy"—of the mid-seventies has diminished. Still, noise
levels in the hallways are very high; during passing period a white
visitor to the school will probably feel unsafe. A dean of discipline
confesses that some parents give their children weapons to protect
themselves at school.

At Central High students read on average at the fourth-grade
level. The few faculty members who care about high academic standards are profoundly gloomy. The best of them are trying to change
careers. The school's administration is a well-meaning and self-protective bureaucracy, at once troubled by declining black faith in the merits
of education and convinced that the school's nonacademic responsibilities supersede its educational tasks. The principal's chief complaint
is the "horrendous" amount of paperwork his office must process in
order to meet federal and state regulations. (His obligations include
drawing up individual lesson plans for all students entitled to remedial
education, testing for bilingual education eligibility, running the free-
lunch program, registering voters in the student body, and keeping detailed records of any disciplinary proceeding.) Complex administrative procedures, accountability standards and instrumental
goals are mandated by Trenton or Washington. Differences within
the faculty create a mosaic of institutional aims and behavioral
norms.

But it is said that no matter how dismal the school, there is
always at least one outstanding instructor working within it. At Central
High that teacher is Fred Pollock. To judge by appearance, he is a
man with a calling. As scholar and raconteur he puts St. Benedict's'
Jack Dalton to shame. In one class (twenty-six enrolled, thirteen attending), he explains slavery and the coming of the Civil War in a
cadent voice that moves the narrative along with relish and precision.
He mentions his own graduate studies on the topic. His hands are

in constant motion. Unlike most of his colleagues, he wears a coat and tie.

After class Pollock's words are unsettling. Behind closed doors, in the teachers' room, he contends that his students tend to respect some teachers much more than is generally believed. What is not respected, he says, is academic content or the life of the mind, not among students, parents, or the faculty. This gifted teacher is angry and depressed by a school that he feels has lost sight of educational substance. "I don't get much satisfaction from teaching," he says. "Here, it is a dead profession in a dead school."

From the Newark example, educational leaders and policy analysts might conclude that they should promote extensive private school options to correct the unacceptable style of much urban education. But the success of urban private schools like St. Benedict's depends a great deal on positive family values toward education and willingness to sacrifice for it. It is doubtful that such attitudes can be made universal or, in the lower class, even conventional. Perhaps school reformers should be content to remember Coleman's counsel to look for ways to make public schools *more* like private ones. And this depends on the increased presence of school-level administrators with sufficient academic interest and authority to copy traits such as those already in place at St. Benedict's:

- *An Academic Curriculum.* At St. Benedict's all students receive a full course of study in the basic subjects. No effort is made to dilute course material to meet the putative "special" needs of disadvantaged pupils.
- *Firm Rules.* The principal and teachers exude care for the impoverished and deprived, but by word and manner they make it clear that they and their vocation are to be respected. No student unnerves or intimidates them. A clear hierarchy exists between adults and children. All students are expected to treat adults as models and superiors. In return, faculty members regard their charges as gentlemen–apprentices and treat them accordingly.
- *High Expectations.* Parents and students, on one side, perceive St. Benedict's as a conduit to a better future. On the other

side, the faculty is firmly convinced that its students can achieve academic and vocational levels commensurate with or superior to those of the Irish, Italian, and Slavic teenagers who attended the school a generation ago. Competition is encouraged. Exacting standards of obedience, courtesy, and honesty prevail.

- *Peer Support.* During the early and continuing initiation into the school's curriculum and code of conduct, each student is assisted by fellow students who have mastered the school's standards and who help younger boys succeed. As a result no student remains isolated in his endeavors. Older students are proud of themselves. They challenge younger boys to match their achievements.
- *Manageable Size.* St. Benedict's' small size tends to create a tight-knit central administration able to monitor students on an individual basis. Students having academic or emotional difficulties cannot remain anonymous. And because of small size, each pupil has high likelihood of achieving some extracurricular distinction.

American education's most profound inequality at present is unequal pupil access to high cognitive and behavioral standards. And many educationists and jurists, in trying to be every child's redeemer, have come to defend a common-school system that sets accepted standards of learning and virtue at the lowest, most abject possible standards. In districts that serve the professional and managerial elites the common-school denominator may remain quite high solely on account of community tastes. But in most districts that service the lower class the denominator falls toward zero. Schools like St. Benedict's inadvertently threaten, illuminating by contrast how much lower-class youth can achieve, given the opportunity.

School improvement does not require acts of God. It requires, instead, that parents and professionals affirm new kinds of common rights. Of whatever race, background, or ability, all children should have the right to attend schools that impose meaningful (and color-blind) standards designed to push them toward their maximum potential. These standards must prevail over more specific—often self-declared—rights of aggrieved groups and antisocial individuals. In most districts, happily, this means only that schools must be less tolerant of careless, lazy, and selfish children (who are often said to be "acting out" obscure psychological problems). In troubled cities schools like St. Benedict's offer obvious models of quality for public schools, models that do not require white or ecclesiastical leadership. Everywhere, reform depends on educators who have the nerve and legal right to set high goals for all students, including the disadvantaged. The question of the eighties is whether or not educational leaders will decide to take up this challenge.

SEVEN

Turning
Toward Basics

A DIFFERENT EDUCATIONAL WIND BLOWS across the land, to be felt in a diverse round of initiatives to impose higher academic standards, more rigorous teaching methods, and better disciplined learning environments. It chills the horde of childsavers and reconstructionists, therapists and emancipators, technicians and certifiers who a few years ago had near-absolute control over the elementary and secondary agenda. No longer do their modern school designs appear exactly to be indisputable betterments. A hundred new pastoral and nonacademic school missions now seem to explain part of the nation's dwindling scholastic productivity. With a speed that has left Progressives stunned or disarmed, a new school reform movement has arrived.

To many of those now making the case for traditional schooling, low achievement is only the tip of an iceberg. Why so much juvenile inactivity and nihilism, they ask? Why are so many young people surly and anxious in free and relaxed school climates? Do the cosmetic reforms of the recent past add up to a massive abdication of adult responsibility? Can schools be anything other than conservative when

114

their essential functions include the disciplined study of received knowledge and the objective ranking of competence?

For some intellectuals there are even larger questions. Do the basic subjects—that is, the bodies of knowledge that include language, mathematics, science, history, and the fine arts—still exert enough authority on their own to capture the attention of youth easily diverted by stimulating but vulgar and character-destroying activities? Could yet another generation largely indifferent to precise thinking and informed judgment inflict irreparable damage on a citizen-propelled polity and information-based economy? In the future should we expect a polarized state inhabited by mechanistic Alphas and bewildered Deltas?

Of course not. But the new reformers—experts and lay public alike—say that school reorganization must then take place to revitalize general knowledge and extend its reach over students. This will not be easy and may be impossible, for everywhere there are images, reputations, budgets, and bureaucracies to protect. But now the problems facing the country's schools have been accurately described and diagnosed. Given a plenitude of research on effective schools, the way to correct much of what is wrong is already known. The question now is how far reformers can go to implement this knowledge.

One of the great ironies in education today is that the relatively neutral term *basic education* provokes such intense passion and controversy. This may be because so many adherents of "the basics" act as if the promotion of elementary skills in reading, writing, and computation is a sufficient educational goal. The term *basic education* was invented by postwar intellectuals, led by Arthur Bestor, who opposed life-adjustment education. For them, like their predecessors Charles W. Eliot and William C. Bagley, the transmission of general knowledge was properly the school's first and central mission. Twenty-five years later the popular slogan *back to basics* displaced an older and more serious educational philosophy. Under this banner gathered those with fervent enthusiasms for competency testing, fundamental schools, and other reductive reforms of dubious value. With them came nostalgics

115

and moralists obsessed with peripheral educational topics such as dress codes, sex education, corporal punishment, and school prayer.

Subsequently, and with some malice, partisan educators and journalists have depicted the basics movement as a faintly dangerous combine of primitives, creationists, tax-resisters, blind patriots, and residual racists. By and large they have missed the point that a much larger group interested in basic education comprises honorable parents, teachers, voters, community leaders, and elected officials genuinely worried about learning outcomes, the quality of juvenile life, deteriorating standards of discipline, and the prevailing attitudes of educational leaders toward all of this.

The back-to-basics movement got under way in the mid-seventies, even as the liberal consensus reached its crest of power. After 1970 newspapers and magazines brimmed with reports of abolished course requirements, breathtaking methodological alterations, and weird campus innovations, all of them ritually described as major educational advances. Simultaneously the press announced soaring levels of delinquency and declining test outcomes, grave problems that these major educational advances would surely reverse. After a time many local leaders, employers, and parents of school-age children decided not. The erosion of academic performance and schoolyard discipline— which many of them witnessed firsthand—seemed tied to the new reforms. They sensed, correctly, that too many children, especially minorities, were being shortchanged on basic skills. Unlike educators influenced by trade reports and publications, these citizens never lost faith in the value of traditional schooling. Between 1974 and 1980, according to national surveys, public confidence in the *value* of education remained exceedingly high. At the same time confidence in school *management and practices* plunged. A spontaneous grassroots movement erupted from the local level, continental in scale, born of lost confidence in the people who controlled the country's public school system.

School boards were first to feel the impact. According to the National School Board Association, by 1978 about 70 percent of U.S. districts had formally discussed the state of basic skills at at least one meeting, about one-quarter of them had changed their curricula at the elementary level to increase time spent on the basic subjects,

116

and another 30 percent were considering such changes. Early on, it was clear that few Washington-based policy-shapers shared these local interests in fundamental cognitive skills. Thus school board activists and civic leaders registered their complaints in state capitals. Elected representatives often responded recklessly. As a result, since 1972 some forty states have enacted minimum competency standards for students or teachers (in many cases both).

Student proficiency testing is at present an exceedingly popular concept. Recent Gallup Polls show that about 80 percent of the public endorses it. The significance of the initiative should escape no professional educator. Minimum competency testing has been imposed by governors, legislators, and other state officials on recalcitrant educational leaders, accurately reflecting the strong feelings and frustrations of public school clients. The enactment of academic competency standards state by state is nothing less than a conscious detour around a national education establishment. The value of the tests is doubtful. Yet these measurements indicate a passionate and persistent belief among the people, and a sound one, in the value of basic academic skills.

State to state student competency tests are used in a variety of ways, always in line with complex regulations and constant legal challenges. They may determine which students receive remedial instruction and which are promoted or graduated. In some cases tests are developed locally; in others tests are adopted by entire states. No two states, in fact, have taken identical action in mandating tests and minimum standards. But in typical situations state lawmakers require a series of language and arithmetic tests, one to be administered before the sixth grade and others to be given at higher grade levels. Each test has a pass–fail "performance floor." The outcome of giving such tests, it is hoped, will be to provide an early warning system for struggling students, some assurance of achievement-based school promotion, or a guarantee that all high school graduates have met specified standards in basic skills. (The required performance level for graduation is often set at the eighth-grade level, meaning that *all* twelfth graders must achieve competencies identical with those of the *average* eighth grader).

To what benefit? Competency standards tend to enable or force

117

schools to concentrate on academic essentials needed for higher learning, even though they are perforce modestly and narrowly defined. They also tend to motivate marginal students who do not take their school work seriously. Proficiency standards tend to call attention as well to the deficiencies of the lowest tenth or quarter of student bodies historically ignored, moved up and out, or shunted into no-effort courses.

At what risk? Like most faddish mandates, proficiency tests are blunt instruments, usually proposed hastily and implemented clumsily. Often their primary motive is to shock, not to reform. Inflexible state codes can in effect reduce local discretionary power. Tests hold students accountable for failure while excusing curriculums, teachers, administrators, school boards, and parents. They are of little use to the very slow and semiretarded and can be very demoralizing for them. And if remedial education means only more of whatever resulted in student failure in the first place, then tests for students who demonstrate early disability are at once a cruel hoax and an early invitation to drop out of school.

The political popularity of competency testing seems based largely on its cut-and-dried quality. Seeking educational goals that are attainable and measurable, state-level political establishments have pressed determinedly for a universal, specified, legally approved educational standard. But such a standard has been pegged to modest language and arithmetic skills (making these proficiency tests better gauges of effective elementary schools than of secondary programs). The competency requirement has then reduced the official goals of schooling, limiting them to low-level cognitive attainments. No longer do the stated aims of schooling include transmitting the cultural heritage, spurring social improvement, and nurturing individual enlightenment. The required end of education, then, is rudimentary literacy as measured by standardized tests, really nothing more.

These are serious reservations. Unfortunately, too many educational leaders have brushed them aside. To try to discredit student competency testing, they have depended on more inflammatory arguments, apparently designed to present competency standards as the work of mischievous and know-nothing reactionaries. Proficiency tests, they claim, discourage higher learning, stifle student and teacher creativity, stir up student resentment, endanger valuable electives in art and music, and humiliate pupils (disproportionately nonwhite). These leaders are probably anxious, too, about the chief embarrassment of competency testing: In the early eighties the large number of nonwhite student failures was revealing how unspeakably low the liberal consensus had set its sights for minority achievement.

Time and again education leaders have tried to evade any external drive for accountability standards that might call attention to individual or group differences. Arguably, this fear of evaluation has contributed to the public impression that a large number of schoolteachers are marginally literate. This notion has spawned a second competency movement to test teachers. By 1982, amid controversies over what should be tested and what to do about the high rate of minority teachers failing the tests, at least eighteen states had proposed or enacted minimum testing standards for people applying for teachers' licenses.

Among legislators and the lay public, as with student testing, such a reform had great appeal, mainly because of its simplicity. Yet the teacher testing drive seemed very ill advised. These state certification tests sought mainly to gauge a prospective teacher's basic skills, that is, ability to read and compute at a high school level. That these skills were even in question should shame those who have decided to award college diplomas and degrees to education majors who might not have them. But it is highly improbable that the number of authentic illiterates among the nation's 2 million instructors is high enough to warrant such tests. "Minimum competency testing of teachers can serve only to single out the most egregiously incompetent—and antagonize or insult the great majority," one knowledgeable test analyst observes.

Teacher evaluation might have more validity if it tried to determine an individual's fitness to deal constructively with children and adolescents, to plan and conduct classes, to encourage reason and decency, to act as a guide to the life of the mind, and so on. One of the true scandals of American educational research is that, after much time and the expenditure of billions, there are not yet any widely agreed-on criteria of what constitutes superior instruction, even though in every school it seems that "everybody knows" who are the best and worst teachers. In any case good teaching includes qualities that a written or multiple-choice test simply cannot identify with precision.

What is testable is a prospective teacher's mastery of specific bodies of knowledge, such as geometry or European history. Mastery tests do make a great deal of sense, then, for those who seek certification in specific subject areas at the secondary level. For this reason, and out of interest in the basic skills, some educational leaders, including AFT President Albert Shanker, support proficiency examinations for teachers before they are hired. Shanker refuses to sanction the testing of hired teachers, however, and the NEA calls the idea of testing prospective *or* hired teachers "indefensible."

As reform instruments, competency tests for students or teachers are expected to produce results that they are incapable of achieving. Student testing, it is felt, will force schools to teach all students academic essentials, set higher standards of achievement, inspire teachers to work harder, require schools to prove their effectiveness, and make diplomas stand for something. Teacher testing, it is felt, will force education departments and schools to manufacture men and women of sterling mind. Needless to say, these are ambitions that are far beyond the power of a simple testing device.

Alongside state-driven competency testing a second, and also defective, back-to-basics initiative has burst forth at the *district* level. Hundreds of localities, responding to parental frustration and pressure, now operate what they call fundamental, traditional, or back-to-basics schools. These alternative schools now operate in fifteen states, in cities from Palo Alto, California, to Philadelphia, Pennsylvania, with notable success at the elementary level, where a structured approach to basic skills makes sense. Such schools are entirely different from selective college preparatory institutions that have long operated at public expense (e.g., departed Townsend–Harris and Dunbar or present-day Stuyvesant, Boston Latin, and Lowell). Children of all capabilities are admitted by parental request. Long waiting lists for entrance confirm the popularity, if not the incontestable superiority, of these basics schools.

But alternative back-to-basics schools raise many questions. Are these special schools salutary reform devices or triumphs of public relations? Traditional schools are said to offer parents and children a "quality" option in the public sector. Yet that option rarely includes much more than the pious celebration of elementary skills and old-time discipline, school practices that thousands of "regular" public schools across the country promote with equal effect and less noise. If traditional schools are in fact more effective, why are they alternatives instead of norms? And in districts where a little "basic" window dressing pacifies confused and unhappy parents, what in the world is going on in "regular" public schools?

The possible pitfalls of the fundamental school movement may be discerned in the case of Pasadena, California. Since mid-century Pasadena has evolved from a prosperous Los Angeles suburb into a semi-independent metropolitan node with a population well over 100,000. And with this change have come certain educational problems usually associated with inner cities. For many years the city's neighborhoods have been highly differentiated by class, outlook, and race. The population includes upper-class conservatives, liberal young professionals and academics, evangelical Christians, fixed-income retirees, and middle-class *and* lower-class nonwhites. In Pasadena the large nonwhite population is descended in part from a servant class; racial prejudice and class resentment are historical facts of local life. A 1969 desegregation order precipitated a cataclysmic white withdrawal from the public schools. (By 1980, in a district where the population was more than 70 percent white, the percentage of white public school students was 32 percent and falling. An estimated 65 percent of the city's white school-age children attended private schools.)

Pasadena's public system once had a deserved reputation for educational excellence. After the 1969 court intervention, however, the district speedily gained double notoriety as a center of grave racial tension *and* reckless educational experimentation. In 1972 the city's liberal school board was displaced by a coalition of conservative citizens led by Henry S. Myers, all worried about school quality, white flight, and real estate values.

After gaining control of the district, Myers and his associates on the school board decided to found one of the nation's first fundamental schools. In September 1973 John Marshall Fundamental School, a combined junior and senior high school, opened with great flourish,

121

long waiting lists, and racial balance. Instantly the school earned wide publicity and praise for its use of letter grades, strict dress codes, no-nonsense curriculum, regular homework assignments, emphasis on character education, and so on. Media reports acted as though such items had disappeared from "regular" schools, which was wrong, but John Marshall's explicit affirmation of them was promising indeed.

A decade after its establishment, Pasadena's prototype is less than a model school. Its energetic and effective first principal has left, replaced by a new head not up to the task of effective school leadership. As other district schools have closed on account of slipping enrollments, teachers indifferent or hostile to the school's principles have become a substantial force on the faculty. No one on the staff can articulate John Marshall's philosophy of education in anything but the crudest clichés.

Student outcomes at Marshall present a mixed picture. At the eighth-grade level, in verbal and mathematical areas students perform not much better than pupils in other district junior high schools. At the tenth-grade level they perform substantially better in reading and writing, but in math they do about the same as students in other district high schools. The reasons for higher achievement can be debated. Some argue that it is because the student body is self-selecting. But the school is full of troubled students whose negligent parents have sent them there to be shaped up. Presumably, Marshall's limited success derives from a *slightly* more rigorous course of study than that at "regular" schools.

From the standpoint of character education the school has had minimal impact. True, white seventh- and eighth-grade students say they like Marshall because they can attend school without fear. Yet truancy rates are very high. Students claim that drug abuse is rampant. A dean maintains that, except among the children of born-again Christians, sexual activity is "near-universal" by the tenth grade.

Why has a school like John Marshall, whose "traditional" bias has some genuine merit, proved disappointing? Some of the blame should fall on the district office, which has not cared for the enterprise. But more, Marshall was created in a crisis atmosphere, with its founders acting in a spirit of self-righteous alarm. It was established as an "outside" challenge to the district, devoid of a developed theory of education or interest in the higher cognitive skills. Myers's ample writing on back-to-basics schools reflects the founder's reductive, back-looking impulses. In his treatises Myers indicates little interest in cognitive analysis, critical thinking, or creative expression. Instead he displays a highly idiosyncratic taste for Tom Swift and McGuffey readers, a fondness for Dale Carnegie–style homilies, an enthusiasm for corporal punishment and spine-tingling patriotic exercises, a weakness for scientific creationism, and a conviction that federal school aid and declining student achievement are inextricably linked. Like many seeking to establish public fundamental schools, Myers does not extend his scholastic interests beyond elementary-level verbal and mathematical skills. And to some his half-avowed moral agenda for the schools is quite offensive.

In the basics movement's simplistic strain there is much to criticize. But instead of trying to sort out the good and the bad in current drives for higher school standards, the education establishment has usually chosen to characterize all proponents of scholastic traditionalism as benighted and bigoted forces menacing hard-won reforms. Too bad. Instead of redirecting its considerable energies in behalf of academic improvement, this establishment has continued to endorse race-conscious measures. It has acted as though its innovations and activities should be regarded as doctrine beyond debate. It has conducted public *autos-da-fé* (at conventions and conferences) in which heretics feared for their careers. In doing so, it has snubbed grassroots sentiment with astonishing arrogance. It has insisted that everything was really just fine and that parents really did not know what was best for their children. In the face of electoral criticism it has reacted with petulance and contempt. Many educational leaders have claimed, unconvincingly, that they have been focused on basics all along, thank you.

In April 1977, for example, a high-level educational conference met at the famous Wingspread estate in Racine, Wisconsin, to examine the state of the basics. Its forty participants included nationally known curricular specialists, legislators, public school administrators, university officials, and educational association directors. Lo and behold, at the end of three days the meeting concluded by proudly restating

123

the *Cardinal Principles,* first enunciated in 1918. An indispensable set of basics, the panel agreed, included education for health and physical fitness, social and civic responsibility, economic capability, creativity, use of leisure, humaneness, and positive self-concept. This was an astonishing end run around the issue at hand: According to the Wingspread participants, *what the schools were already doing was the very essence of the basics.* Here, there was no affirmation of scholarship, no case for standards of excellence, no admission of wrong directions, no desire to streamline school operations. There was no celebration of cognition, ratiocination, thinking. There were, instead, the same tired bromides, more whitewash, more self-deception, more evidence of programmatic bankruptcy in education's reigning elites.

Not all progressive educators have been as complacent as those who met at Wingspread. In early 1978 Christopher Jencks, author of *Inequality,* summarized his objections to the back-to-basics movement in *The Washington Post.* Refreshingly, unlike the Wingspread gang, Jencks did not try to justify the current condition of elementary and secondary schools. And in his extremely intelligent review he signaled some unintended comradeship with conservative intellectuals also alarmed by qualitative school decay.

Jencks criticized the basic movement's tendency to focus on the state of elementary learning. "Where problems appear, they are with more complex skills, with the students' desire or ability to reason, with lack of interest in ideas, with a shortage of information about the world around them," he said. "If schools need to do anything today—and it is doubtful that schools can alone solve the problem—it is to get back to complexity, not to basics."

In trying to explain the learning crisis, Jencks first rejected the claims of those who said that standardized tests fail to measure student reasoning skills, are biased against lower-class students, or stress obscure and irrelevant operations. He also discounted (rather too briskly) such developments as desegregation, declining academic requirements, grade inflation, changes in family structure, and television. To explain the problem, Jencks landed on adult uncertainty, sensitivity to juvenile opinion, doubts about traditional standards, and unwillingness to

124

coerce or punish students. "The life of the mind requires that one have a certain disrespect for those in authority, that one remain loyal to one's own notion of rationality even when authorities do not share it," he said. "Trouble arises, however, when people lose respect for external authority without developing any internalized standards of their own."

In the sixties, Jencks went on, it seemed that rationality itself was nothing but an illusion. "There seemed to be so many competing interpretations of reality that it was hard to defend one to the exclusion of others. This led not only students but many teachers into the kind of spongy cultural relativism that treats all ideas as equally defensible. But if all ideas are equally defensible, none is worth bothering with." The central defects in the basics movement, Jencks concluded, were its concern with areas of the curriculum that are not deteriorating and "with restoring respect for persons in authority, like parents and teachers, and not for ideas."

Jencks underestimated the seriousness of lapsed adult authority. But in making the case for general knowledge, academic rigor, and intellectual substance, the erstwhile radical was not distant from the lineal descendants of Bagley and Bestor, also troubled by retrogressive and anti-intellectual tendencies in the basics movement. These were the "basic education" scholars long associated with the subject-centered philosophy, educational luminaries including Jacques Barzun, James D. Koerner, and George Weber. Educational conservatives had long insisted that schools should require an academic course of study for virtually all students, advancing students on the basis of scholastic achievement, employing adults devoted to high cognitive standards, and eschewing new techniques, materials, subjects, and programs urged in spite of questionable validity and value.

What Essentialists lacked before now was sufficient political thrust to make these sentiments conventional. Open classrooms, performance contracting, values clarification, pass–fail, death education, and a host of other innovative ideas have lost their cachet. But so far, when they have disappeared, the first cause has not been resurgent traditionalism. More often the termination of federal or foundation seed money, the appearance of a new superintendent or school board, or lack of enthusiasm after an early burst of support has contributed to an innovation's demise. Attempts to end social promotion have met with mixed success, district by district, mainly because of violent controversies swirling around what to do with overage children held back, especially if they are minority students. There has been some jumping up and down about stiffer diploma requirements and more demanding teacher education programs, but to date substantive alterations are few.

The best of the basics movement is grounded in precepts once considered out of date, socially irresponsible, or hard-hearted: that schools should concentrate on promoting general knowledge and academic mastery; that schools are not competent or able to wipe out poverty, eradicate all differences in individual ability, stamp out racial conflict, and counteract family indiscipline; that schools work best when educational policy is developed in decentralized, nonlitigious, school-level settings; that schools should do less, and do what they do better.

Schools cannot succeed at everything. And in broadening their social mission decade by decade, many of them have overloaded their institutional circuits. As a result they can do nothing well, not even convey essential knowledge. Appalled by this state of affairs, an eclectic group of school reformers in districts, state capitals, and Washington is on the move. For all their differences in style and rhetoric, many responsible Progressives, traditionalists, and elected officials now see the connection between continuing national welfare and ongoing investment in human capital. These citizens perceive accelerating technological change that threatens a large portion of the work force impatient with or flustered by complex ideas and meticulous standards. They feel that efficient and vigorous national institutions depend on a public spirit prizing personal accomplishment, conscientiousness, and initiative. By setting larger store by these values, they are convinced, the nation's melancholy and apprehensive mood could diminish. In short, the belief that schools securing academic knowledge and discipline promote a secure future is now a point where many political persuasions converge.

Just a decade or so ago educational leaders interested in the definition and promotion of institutional excellence had become scattered. Ignored or admonished at meetings and conferences, scorned by leading educational associations, and denied access to most professional

126

and popular journals, those who held steadfastly to traditional scholastic methods and goals traveled a lonely road. No longer. Today persuasive new research suggests without much doubt that schools *do* make a difference and that schools *are* reformable. And quality-minded reformers are acting on that information. This is, of course, the genuine good news of the eighties.

EIGHT

What Makes
an Effective School

A QUIET REVOLUTION is taking place in thought about schools, one that gives every appearance of dropping the curtain on the era of pessimism and despair the early Coleman and Jencks reports ushered in. In recent years school research has concentrated not on *what* human, institutional, and financial resources are available in schools but on *how well* available resources are organized and used. As a result, two heartening views about schools are gaining increased credibility.

The first holds that pupil achievement is not foreordained by heredity or neighborhood but is in fact powerfully influenced by what happens in school. The second maintains that what happens in school is susceptible to purposeful alteration and improvement through means largely within the control of those who teach in and manage the schools. To use the words of the University of London child psychologist Michael Rutter in describing these fresh lines of reasoning, a consensus is emerging that "schools can do much to foster good behavior and attainments, and that even in a disadvantaged area, schools can be a force for the good." What Rutter says will not greatly surprise many parents and school officials who never thought otherwise. But

128

for many educational leaders, who spent a decade or more scaling down their hopes for schools, this view stands in sharp contrast to the past.

During the sixties education's reigning elites were not exactly indifferent to matters of school improvement. But they tended to measure effectiveness—and their own programmatic success—with quantitative indices, for example, high school retention and graduation rates, the proportion of teachers holding advanced degrees, the amount of money spent per pupil, and the number of court-enforced rights held by individuals and groups. To those who said that these were naive or false gauges of quality, barely related to the internal intellectual life of schools, most educationists turned deaf ears. Then came the Coleman Report in 1966, which said that indeed these measures had negligible impact on outcomes. Suddenly the euphoric reform spirit of the early sixties began to give way to a gloomy social determinism and intensifying interest in free-form educational theories.

Now this cloud cover is beginning to lift. The major foundations, the leading graduate schools of education, and the most influential public and private research institutions are newly hospitable to and cheerful about efforts to improve school quality. The most exciting school research now under way centers on topics such as the propagation of excellence, the definition of standards, the hows and whys of academic mastery, the advancement of juvenile self-discipline, the means of faculty improvement, and the redesign of the curriculum. A new round of studies, projects, and initiatives shows alertness to the school's *educational* function. What is happening—not on education's lunatic fringe but in its establishment's most powerful and august corridors—is a quality-based revolution that may well have a profound impact on the national education agenda for the remainder of the century.

For this nascent school effectiveness movement, we have to thank the handful of isolated researchers who in large part triggered it. These were scholars who during the seventies shied away from the tumultuous debate over the degree to which schools can lessen economic and social inequalities. Instead they began to explore how well schools carried out the functions they were designed for, that is, the extent to which schools could promote academic mastery and decent behavior.

129

And for these analysts one question was central: What, if anything, can schools do to intensify this power? Three pioneering studies stand out: the Weber report on inner-city reading programs, the Bennett comparative review of progressive and traditional teaching styles, and the Rutter survey of secondary school practices and outcomes. Each of them deserves recapitulation.

WEBER

In 1970 a Council for Basic Education analyst, George Weber, spurned the then fashionable explanations for the academic deficiencies of youngsters from low-income families. For Weber, the claim that low student achievement in impoverished urban areas was a simple function of unsatisfactory family backgrounds and inadequate school resources lacked fullness. If he could find inner-city elementary schools where reading achievement was much higher than in other downtown schools, Weber asserted, his "study would show that inner-city children can be taught reading well, and it might discover some common factors in the success of good programs."

Weber chose to investigate third-grade programs because whatever reading methods were used, in whatever elementary schools, by the end of third grade most students are expected to have mastered certain basic mechanical skills. Such skills are a foundation, enabling pupils in fourth grade and above to branch into the study of vocabulary, grammar, composition, and literature. From an initial field of ninety-five schools, Weber selected four—two in New York City, one in Kansas City, and one in Los Angeles—that met his precise standards. Each was a nonselective public school attended by very poor children (determined by Title I and free lunch criteria). In each school the third-grade classes achieved reading scores equal to or higher than the national norm and contained an unusually low percentage of non-readers.

After administering his own tests and making extended school visits, Weber reviewed the qualities in these four schools that seemed to account for superior outcomes. All of them, he found, benefited from forceful administrators, high facultywide expectations for student achievement, and an orderly school atmosphere. In all the reading programs there was schoolwide concern about reading skills, adroit use of reading specialists, a phonics-based curriculum, attention to individual student reading interests, and careful evaluation of pupil progress. Just as important, Weber identified several school characteristics often said to be crucial to high levels of student achievement that were *not* universal in the four schools studied: small class size, ability grouping, exceptional teachers, school personnel of the same ethnic background as the students', preschool education, and outstanding physical facilities.

Like others before him, Weber correlated reading achievement and pupil backgrounds. He noted that the four successful inner-city schools had academic attainments approximately *equal* to schools serving average-income students but *below* schools serving high-income students. As a group, Weber contended, children from affluent homes had higher average intelligence. (Not because of race or ethnic background, he said. All-white schools also exhibited average student ability levels in direct relation to average parental wealth.) Weber, surmising the academic advantages of well-to-do children, noted that they tend to come from homes where reading is a part of daily life, where parents introduce their children to reading well before school-starting age, where more available reading materials exist, and where home conditions are more conducive to reading. But, he stressed, these nonschool forces were not overwhelming determinants of performance; if they were, school attainment would *always* correlate with them. Not all schools were equally effective, Weber concluded in a prototypical statement that later, larger and more ambitious studies would embellish. But schools attended by disadvantaged youngsters could be effective.

When Weber's study was completed in 1971, his findings made their way onto the front page of *The New York Times.* Today his work is considered a seed of later school effectiveness research. But only now are analysts paying great attention to this early foray. In the era of Silberman and Jencks, when the study appeared, the Weber report could not single-handedly roll back two powerful tides, one moving against schools as nurseries of intellect, another against schools as engines of social and economic mobility. Not surprisingly, in a time when effective school methods, systematic aims, and high standards were widely regarded as dehumanizing, discriminatory, or meaningless, many educational leaders greeted the Weber report with indifference bordering on hostility.

BENNETT ET AL.

In 1976 a quite different effectiveness study appeared. The British researcher Neville Bennett and his colleagues at the University of Lancaster had set out four years earlier to determine the relative merits of different elementary-level teaching styles: Did different teaching styles result in different rates of pupil progress? Did different types of pupils perform better under certain styles of teaching? The researchers approached the study with an acknowledged bias toward informal or open classrooms (which they defined as "progressive education, admittedly dressed slightly differently and wearing a trendy new name"). They were distressed, however, by "innovation being implemented, not on research evidence, but on faith," and sought to rectify the situation.

The Bennett team administered surveys to third- and fourth-grade teachers and pupils in some 750 Lancashire and Cumbria schools. From these it built a typology of teaching styles ranging from the highly progressive to highly traditional (see Table 8–1). Later, to correlate the reactions of different pupil personalities to different teaching styles, the study created a student typology. Then the researchers selected thirty-seven teachers using several different instructional styles and, at the beginning and end of the 1973–74 academic year, tested each of their classes for cognitive and affective outcomes.

Bennett was shocked by what he found. In every variable tested, traditional methods resulted in greater learning. Why? According to the researchers, because enormous classroom variations existed in the time students spent working on subject matter. In more traditional classrooms, where teachers stressed academic attainment and the acquisition of basic skills, there tended to be more of this "time-on-task." The more time spent on subject matter, the study determined, the greater the likelihood of pupil progress. This homely finding was matched by some more surprising results. Pupils in progressive class-

132

TABLE 8–1
Progressive and Traditional Styles

PROGRESSIVE	TRADITIONAL
1. Integrated subject matter	Separate subject matter
2. Teacher as guide to educational experiences	Teacher as distributor of knowledge
3. Active pupil role	Passive pupil role
4. Pupils participate in curriculum planning	Pupils have no say in curriculum planning
5. Learning predominantly by discovery techniques	Accent on memory, practice, and rote
6. External rewards and punishments not necessary, i.e., intrinsic motivation	External rewards used (e.g., grades), i.e., extrinsic motivation
7. Not too concerned with conventional academic standards	Concerned with academic standards
8. Little testing	Regular testing
9. Accent on cooperative group work	Accent on competition
10. Teaching not confined to classroom base	Teaching confined to classroom base
11. Accent on creative expression	Little emphasis on creative expression

Source: Reprinted by permission from Neville Bennett et al., *Teaching Styles and Pupil Progress,* Harvard University Press, 1976.

rooms that emphasized self-expression *did not* evince greater imagination or creativity than their formally instructed counterparts. Also, insecure and timid students tended to work harder and better in traditional classrooms. Finally, in informal classrooms the ablest students were often the pupils whose scholastic performance suffered the most. According to the Bennett study, not only did progressive methods hinder the transmission of skills of literacy and computation, but they did not even compensate for this loss by encouraging creativity or helping ill-adjusted children. As the psychologist Jerome Bruner put it in a foreword to Bennett's work, "Inadvertently, informal classrooms are academic levelers, though it was thought they would allow all to proceed at their own pace. They also—again inadvertently—hurt most the less well-adjusted student, who, it was thought, would be the most helped."

Bennett did not leap to sweeping antiprogressive conclusions or make elaborate recommendations. He made mention of the success of informal techniques in the hands of ingenious teachers and noted that progressive methods tended to increase student motivation. Instead of Prussian drill, he prescribed a less nebulous, ambiguous adult presence in elementary classrooms. He called for increased emphasis on curricular definition, planning, and direction. Classroom settings can be informal, Bennett suggested, without being ineffectual. But to him, adult beliefs that pupils are able to guide themselves in meaningful ways were theoretically unsound and potentially harmful.

This report dealt a blow to the open classroom concept. Bennett chided Silberman especially for vituperating against formal and traditional methods in the absence of sound data or evidence to back up his case. He warned:

> On both sides of the Atlantic innovation is being urged without research. This of course is not new in education, the common response being that educational decisions cannot afford to wait for years while careful trials are instituted and evaluated. Yet it is a strange logic which dictates that we *can* afford to implement changes in organization and teaching which have unknown, and possibly, deleterious effects on the education of the nation's young.

RUTTER ET AL.

The Weber and Bennett studies tell us much about the identification and promotion of school effectiveness. But they and a number of other recent investigations into school style only set the stage for a study of secondary schools that many now regard as a modern landmark in school research, *Fifteen Thousand Hours*. Since the results of this meticulous seven-year longitudinal study appeared in 1979, enlightened thinking in educational circles has shifted abruptly. Part of the reason is that Rutter's work goes a long way to establish that schools have an emphatic impact on child development and that the characteristics of the school a pupil attends can matter a great deal.

The background of the study is interesting. At the beginning of the seventies Michael Rutter was unconvinced by a flurry of reports that stressed the meager influence of schools on pupil attainments and behavior. If not school, then what? Was it family, heredity, luck, the economic and political structure of society, or something else? Rutter was puzzled at the amount of scholarly disagreement on the topic and annoyed by the clashing data, methods, and formulations that different researchers were using to make their points. In addition he felt that many large-scale studies had examined a very narrow range of variables to determine school effects, for example, tested verbal achievement or average expenditure per pupil, the number of books in the school library, or the teacher–pupil ratio.

Previous research had already revealed great variations in such school conditions. There was a near-absence of information, however, on what students were like before they faced these variables and on the effect of different school conditions on different students. Rutter argued that most researchers had simply ignored the internal life of schools, that is, the differences in institutional atmosphere, climate, values, and habits that constitute what Rutter called the school's ethos. A psychologist and not a sociologist by trade, Rutter suspected that variations in ethos would in large part explain glaring differences in student attainment and character.

Through the seventies Rutter and his associates followed 2,700 London students from the end of elementary school through twelve secondary schools, all of them nonselective and containing a large number of low-income and minority pupils. They gauged cognitive and behavioral outcomes in terms of school attendance rates, the proportion of students remaining in school beyond the legally enforced age, success on national achievement tests, and the incidence of delinquency.

In trying to make the link between outcomes and practices, Rutter's mode of investigation was clever, his items of inspection novel. During class visits, for instance, Rutter and his colleagues recorded the amount of student work displayed on walls, noted whether home-

135

work was regularly assigned and promptly marked, and calculated how much time was spent on and off task. When the researchers handed out pupil questionnaires, they noted how many youngsters had to borrow pencils. Among other things, they asked students to report how often they used the school library for enjoyment, how often they were punished (e.g., scolded, detained, smacked), how often they were rewarded (e.g., given prizes), how often they participated in assembly programs, and how often they went on field trips. Teachers were asked to describe their school's and their own homework policies and to state their expectations for students. "Is anyone aware if staff arrive late for school?" they were asked. "Do you have adequate clerical help?"

Some of Rutter's findings corroborated things Coleman and others had established years before: On the average, middle-class students outperform lower-class students in school; compared to families, schools are weak social institutions; to create an effective school, a core of able students may be a necessary prerequisite; and in fostering superior outcomes, some resource differences among schools, such as the age of the physical plant or the size of classes, are of negligible importance.

But according to Rutter's sophisticated analysis the internal life or ethos of schools has great bearing on pupil success. Students of low ability entering the "best" schools, for example, had exam results equal to those of high-ability pupils entering the "worst" schools. At two different schools, one-third of the entering boys at the age of ten were identified as difficult and potentially troublesome. Four years later the actual delinquency rate for the same boys attending one school was five times as high as that for the boys attending the other school. A school's ethos, Rutter asserted, like a tide carrying all boats, affects the level of scholarship and conduct of all students, causing the norm to rise or fall. Individual differences do not vanish, but certain variables tend to pull average student performance up, and others tend to pull it down. The study concluded:

> First our investigation clearly showed that secondary schools varied markedly with respect to their pupils' behavior, attendance, exam success and delinquency. This had been observed before, but the demonstration that these differences remained *even after taking*

into account differences in their intake [that is, student backgrounds and presecondary records, Rutter's emphasis] was new. Secondly, we found that these variations in outcome were systematically and strongly associated with the characteristics of schools as social institutions.

What made for a positive ethos and therefore an effective school? In good schools, Rutter said, adults and children alike seemed to take school seriously. Principals, department heads, and senior staff set and monitored well-defined standards for their teachers. And faculty members acted self-consciously as models of mental and moral probity. They prepared their classes, were punctual, did not waste time in class, and rarely ended lessons early. They also held high expectations for their students and showed these concerns by assigning homework and explicitly rewarding industry. In good schools it did not matter much that school codes differed. It was far more important that normative regulations existed and were enforced fairly, with uniform penalties for those who failed to meet school standards. Not unexpectedly, in return, students tended to imitate the models of school adults, copying the purposeful attitudes of authority figures, straining to perform at capacity, and trying to live up to what was expected of them.

At first glance, Rutter admitted, these conclusions seemed modest, even obvious. "After all, it is scarcely surprising that children benefit from attending schools which set good standards, where teachers provide good models of behavior, where they are praised and given responsibility, where the general conditions are good and where the lessons are well conducted," he said. But Rutter then pointed out that it would have been equally "obvious" had his research shown that the most important factors in school success were small school size with a favorable teacher–student ratio, an extensive guidance and welfare support-system, faculty continuity, and severe punishment in cases of misdemeanor. In fact, the Rutter study found that *none of these items contributed significantly* to the improvement of student achievement.

We may be tempted to question the applicability of Rutter's findings to U.S. high schools. In *Fifteen Thousand Hours,* time and again we encounter the enormous cultural differences between England and

America. At the secondary level residual ideals of selective schooling—classical, rigorous, and austere—still exert near-universal influence on the British system. For example, when Rutter notes the benefits of relatively relaxed regulations, he nonetheless assumes that most students, even in the grittiest neighborhoods of inner London, wear school uniforms. When he advises the use of rewards and less-than-severe penalties, he still takes corporal punishment to be part of the schoolhouse's natural order.

In reading Rutter it should be remembered, too, that English educators and children have less elaborate senses of individual entitlement than their American counterparts. Civil libertarians and child advocates in Britain have erected fewer constraints on discretionary educational authority. As a result, internal consensus over school standards and goals, which Rutter regards as a prerequisite to the effectiveness of schools, is much harder for U.S. educators to achieve. On the matter of school size Rutter's conclusions may even be plain wrong when applied to the case of American reform. But then, the Rutter study is not the final word. Its importance lies largely in the amount of controversy, debate, and attention it has drawn—and the new projects it has influenced or helped to spawn.

Among school experts the properties of effective schools are not a new topic of debate. The primary contribution of the Weber, Bennett, and Rutter studies has been to begin to base that debate on hard evidence rather than untested theory. Each has provided models for later educational researchers who have reached complimentary and consistent conclusions. They have convinced some school leaders that students' outcomes are not uncontrollable. Reflecting this, an increasing number of American school analysts are pursuing new kinds of research and trains of thought. These include the definition of educationally sound schools for the urban poor, the identification of wholesome educational climates, and, especially at the secondary level, the advocacy of new practices.

The researchers W. B. Brookover, L. W. Lezotte, Jere Brophy, Ronald Edmonds, and others have completed small-scale studies of

138

inner-city school effectiveness. Adopting Weber's technique of identifying highly successful urban schools and then comparing them with less satisfactory schools with similar student populations, these analyses have yielded results that appear to validate most of Weber's findings. A Brookover and Lezotte study, to cite just one example, examined six "improving" and two "declining" urban schools. The researchers concluded that many poor children were deprived of an adequate education because their teachers believed that such students were uneducable, holding low expectations for them that ultimately became a self-fulfilling prophecy. In "improving" schools, by contrast, high expectations were the norm. Because findings such as these have been replicated again and again in authoritative studies of urban schools, something of a consensus is developing about the essential elements of effective schooling. According to researchers, effectual inner-city (and presumably all) schools are likely, in spite of eccentricities and individual differences, to exhibit the following traits:

- *Schoolwide Emphasis on Cognitive Learning.* In superior schools academic learning takes precedence over all other school activities. Class time is considered a precious commodity. Among faculty members there is consensus that any complex learning depends on pupil mastery of low-level skills, and therefore unrelenting attention to the progress of all students in the essentials of reading, writing, and computation. And for all students the objective is higher cognitive development and more advanced knowledge.
- *High Expectations.* In effective schools no student is allowed to fall below a minimum level of achievement without failing. But no child is written off as uneducable, and teachers regard student failure as a challenge to try different methods and techniques. While expected levels of achievement may differ for individual pupils, school staffs genuinely believe that *all* students can master low-level skills and use them to grasp the rudiments of history, civics, and science. Pupil progress, these

139

staffs feel, is not wholly dependent on home environment, parental support, or student temperament.

- *Orderly Classrooms and Campuses.* In well-managed classes the accent is on classroom procedures and routines (e.g., posted schedules) that minimize time-off-task. Teachers give clear and quiet directions, tend to work with the whole class at the same time, and convey a sense of regularity to their students. Outside of class school staffs require students to behave courteously and to meet reasonable standards of hygiene and dress. Obnoxious or violent behavior is not tolerated.
- *Strong Leadership.* In good schools the principal and department heads act as fierce guardians of instructional quality. By standing for high academic outcomes, they provide guidance, too, for teachers, whom they try to select specially in spite of union and bureaucratic pressures. These administrators are willing to be unpopular, if necessary, in the cause of responsible schooling. They tend not to be permissive, informal in their staff relationships, or overly interested in public relations (though the best of them have excellent public relations).
- *Frequent Monitoring and Evaluation.* In exemplary schools tests, grades, and reports are used to assess pupil progress and faculty effectiveness. School staffs are not hostile to the concept of accountability and accept responsibility for educating their students. They do not reject the validity of test scores, even when results are disappointing. Rather, they use test outcomes to decide what is and what is not working in the curriculum. In such an atmosphere teachers do not feel that they are or should be beyond evaluation.

These five general elements can be said to apply equally to effective city, suburban, and rural schools and to both elementary and secondary grades. But they have been noted chiefly through studies of urban elementary schools. Effective schooling at the secondary level raises further issues, since differences in pupil ability, motivation, and character become more pronounced, and subject matter becomes more complex and varied.

To date the most thorough large-scale analysis of effective and ineffective American high schools comes from James S. Coleman's 1981 report, Coleman II, ostensibly a comparison of private and public school practices and outcomes, a report that gained instant notoriety on account of its explicit advocacy of private education. It was the education historian Diane Ravitch who first conceived the report as a "major addition to school effectiveness research," not as an attack on public education or a case for vouchers. How come? *For the same type of student coming from the same background,* Coleman found, average achievement was higher for those who attended private schools. Thus, like Rutter—and in striking contrast to his findings fifteen years earlier—Coleman concluded that *educational policies made a significant difference in student achievement.*

What made the private schools studied* on the average more effective? The short answer, Coleman said, is that private schools are able and willing to enforce exacting requirements, manifest in a rigorous core curriculum, limited elective choice, and substantial homework. Compared to 34 percent of public school students, 70 percent of private school students were on an academic track. And private school students could not readily substitute easy courses for hard ones. Before graduation, as a result, they were more likely to have completed courses in geometry and advanced algebra, chemistry and physics, and foreign language. Also, for private school students, more substantial homework assignments paid the double bonus of increasing time-on-task and linking student home lives to school activity.

In private schools, Coleman found, faculty members were more willing to put pressure on students to make them meet clearly defined standards. Generally, private school educators thought that teachers should initiate student learning, that academic learning is necessary for all students, and that teachers can force students to learn. The greatest difference between private and public schools was the former's more rigorous disciplinary climate. According to Coleman, private schools took decisive action when students endangered their academic attainments (e.g., through class-cutting or truancy) or community stability (e.g., through self-destructive or antisocial behavior). Paradoxi-

* Coleman's only large private high school sample consisted of Catholic schools. His non-Catholic schools were few in number and by common agreement generated few statistically valid comparisons.

141

cally, or maybe not, private school students also reported a *much* higher rate of teacher interest in their welfare, problems, and development than students in public schools.

The Coleman findings and other school-effectiveness research pertain primarily to cognitive achievement. But for another, smaller group of scholars, the root educational reform issue is something else, namely, how to establish strong moral foundations in schools. For these analysts, learning outcomes—and much more—depend on the school's position as a moral agency, an institution with the authority and ability to exercise benign ethical judgments that children will honor and imitate.

Leading theorists of traditional character education, notably Gerald Grant of Syracuse University and Edward Wynne of the University of Illinois, reject academic proficiency as the primary aim of schooling. More precisely, they conceive of the school's moral and intellectual spheres as inseparable. For them the tested cognitive capability of schools is an incomplete and secondary gauge of school quality, offering no evidence of satisfactory behavioral outcomes. "We have too frequently reduced talk about good schools to talk about effectiveness," complains Grant. "We no longer seem to recall Aristotle's language of intellectual and moral virtues; we speak only of a reductionist version of intellectual virtue, as reflected in standardized tests."

Since *Fifteen Thousand Hours* appeared, Grant and Wynne, working independently, have attempted to step beyond Rutter's description of a good school ethos in order to identify the methods and means by which moral institutions can be established. In essence, Grant and Wynne are asking how schools that instill moral habits and build ethical character can be created and sustained. During the 1979–80 school year Grant and his assistants surveyed thirty-three public and private schools scattered throughout the Northeastern states and selected five of them for yearlong studies. To illustrate the properties of good schools, Wynne relied on 167 surveys of Chicago-area schools conducted by his graduate students between 1972 and 1979.

Unsavory institutional, community, and legal forces are cutting at the public school's ability to exercise authority as a moral agency, Grant says. By way of explanation he cites the following alterations in the daily life of schools during the last dozen or so years: (1) *dispersed*

142

authority, which results when new legions of educational specialists, technicians, counselors, and aides issue conflicting commands from a variety of relatively independent school offices, each group all the while engaged in status competition with other groups within the school; (2) *leveled authority,* in which traditional adult freedoms have been radically circumscribed and juvenile rights vastly expanded; and (3) *codified authority,* highly legalistic, rational, and technical in nature, whereby most questions of character, value, and desirable conduct have been ruled out of institutional bounds.

At the extremes, Grant contends, these changes have resulted in substantial reduction of the school's capacity to make judgments to promote the common good. Consistent policies, norms, and traditions are difficult or impossible to arrive at. Students and adults are seen by many as equals quarreling over individual rights, each pursuing private moralities that are—and must be—tolerated so long as no laws are broken. Schools then operate under the assumption, often incorrect, that their members have been educated in decency and in how to act toward others outside the rule of law. Effective schools, says Grant, must induct young members of a community into a set of honorable standards, beliefs, and values. Where no public morality is definable—where values such as altruism, service, effort, and truth are voluntary—he warns, "we are headed for ever greater stress, instability, and perhaps the eventual abandonment of the public schools."

Therefore, like Coleman, Grant supports the introduction of voucher systems that would give credits to parents, allowing them to choose and pay for their children's education in the market place. Both scholars believe that credits to stimulate private alternatives and sidestep public school bureaucracies are needed, but for slightly different reasons. Coleman stresses that education policy now tends to protect the lowest-performing schools and harm the children of the poor. Grant is more bothered by public policy that stimulates an adversarial and necessarily value-neutral school climate. He advises the expanded state support for private institutions grimly, mainly because he feels that in many localities the restoration of a consensual and upright public morality is beyond hope.

Wynne deals less with the nature of school authority and more with beneficial moral practices observed in both public and private schools. According to Wynne, certain traditional institutional arrangements tend to activate the good manners and diligence that parents want their children to learn, the kindness and tact that students want their classmates to possess, and the honesty and altruism that faculty members want their pupils to relish. Through extensive illustrations Wynne depicts the advancement of such moral climates through the recognition, stimulation, and protection of superior conduct. Wynne concludes:

- Good schools value and reward exemplary behavior by giving it a place in the sun. They make frequent awards, give gold and silver stars, issue certificates, present trophies, and bestow special privileges on students who excel. School bulletins announce individual and group achievements. Student accomplishments are celebrated at special assemblies, banquets, and ceremonies.
- Good schools encourage student spirit through songs, class symbols, and intramural competition. They exhort students to participate in charitable fund-raising and volunteer work. They expect students to lend a hand in school maintenance. In such schools, academic effort, cooperation, and self-restraint are regarded as "cool." Cynicism, precocity, and insolence are not.
- Good schools refuse to condone or conceal indiscipline. Their behavior and dress codes serve notice to students and the community that character-destroying behavior will meet official disapproval and penalties. Faculty members try to shield students from fear, uncertainty, and temptation, in part by taking a chary view of the rights of juvenile miscreants. Perhaps most important, in good schools, when parents or students claim (possibly with reason) that a teacher has acted ill-advisedly, rashly, or even extralegally to enforce a decorous school climate, the administration tries its utmost to stand behind its faculty member.

Significantly, interest in effective schools has moved well beyond the academy. Along with researchers, the public is suddenly interested in cognitive and moral development. Much more than military preparedness, national surveys tell us, the American people consider a first-rate educational system crucial to the nation's future security. Add to this the widespread and accurate sense of parents, taxpayers, voters, and elected officials that an unacceptably large number of schools do not meet reasonable standards. Add then new research that is trying to discover and describe the essential qualities of instructionally effective schools. In all of this lie the volcanic possibilities of a still strengthening school reform movement.

A convergence of research findings now provides a surprisingly clear-cut and strikingly old-fashioned model for school reform. A large body of literature, not quite definitive but certainly persuasive, reveals what kind of learning environments, leadership styles, ethical codes, and institutional habits promote effective schools. It indicates that if schools are to be at their best, they should reduce their nonacademic missions and concentrate on cognitive goals. It suggests that private schools are valuable reform paradigms, not because of their "privateness" but because of their clearer scholastic focus and greater scope of authority. Taken as a whole, the new reform findings signify situations we can alter. They may herald an era newly congenial to learning, a time to repair the damage.

The list of prescriptive reform projects recently completed or still under way is impressive. Last year the philosopher Mortimer J. Adler and a panel of distinguished education experts produced a manifesto called *The Paideia Proposal*. It called for nothing less than a universal academic course of study as a precondition to a working democratic state, giving all citizens access to the acquisition of organized knowledge, the development of intellectual skills, and the enlarged understanding of ideas and values. A federal education commission has called for more traditional, academic schooling. The National Academy of Education has planned a report to enumerate essential national values and scholastic standards, along with the necessary changes in school operations to sustain both. In the works is a mammoth effort by the College Board to develop "preferred patterns of preparation" and a set of fundamental competencies for all college-bound students. With generous Carnegie funds behind them, former U.S. Education Commissioner Ernest H. Boyer and former Harvard education dean Theodore R. Sizer have undertaken two different but complementary high school studies, both of which promise to make elaborate recommendations for secondary-level improvements. What this current array of projects seems likely to do is provide some general agreement on two reform topics long and conspicuously absent from the education debate: what standards schools *should* enforce and what students *ought* to learn.

Whatever the specific answers, educational meliorism during the eighties will almost assuredly concentrate on establishing stricter modes of instruction, more exacting courses of study, and less indulgent behavioral codes. It may expect parents and children to cooperate more in achieving high outcomes and to act less as torpid and passive educational consumers. It may reverse long-term trends to deplore "tough" and "traditional" school programs. To be sure, it could turn out that confused, soporific, and self-protective groups of bureaucrats and educators will resist rational change so fully that the private sector will have to be the primary site of reform. Yet more than at any time in recent memory the educational moment seems to be cause for mild optimism.

NINE

Reform
and Its Barriers

No ONE PRETENDS THAT schools by themselves can create republics of virtue. But of all our social agencies they have the possibility of being organized in such ways as to advance the quality of intellectual and civic life. And progressive reformers of several decades have done schools no service by confusing the pleasant and the necessary, the esthetic and the effective, the hypothetical and the attainable.

In coming years authentic school improvement requires more retroflexive thinking, that is, renewed receptiveness to historical models of effectual school methods and aims. The meaning of innovation must be reconsidered so that, for example, the reintroduction of demerit systems and physics courses might be seen as beneficial and truly progressive. It should be understood that because children tend to check constantly the stream of what they say, think, and do against established authority, certain openly stated absolutes are in their interest. It must be taken as basic that holding pupils to high standards does not obviate compassion.

Educational progress now requires the hospitality of educators

147

to scholastic arrangements—say, homework, honest grading, demanding courses, required classes, earned promotion—long maligned or discredited. Above all, reform depends on the resolve of a cadre of educators in each school district, holding a simple canon: that schools provide a great, unique, and sufficient social service when they convey to the great majority of youth the skills of communication and numeration, a sense of past and origins, a recognition of what and where they are, and a concern and respect for rationality. When schools stand unequivocally for values of curiosity, kindness, honesty, and industry, they provide a *locus virtutis* for children and the community. Schools can and, when possible, should try to provide other services. But any activity that impairs, undercuts, or disparages these essential tasks must be opposed and checked.

Acting on this canon cannot and will not be easy, especially for administrators on the front lines. The school boards, superintendents, and principals who in concert try to determine district standards are buffeted daily by countless cacophonous voices, each with policy designs of its own. Huge metropolitan districts are Towers of Babel. The larger the district, the greater the likelihood that union representatives and political action committees, advocacy groups, government inspectors, and court officials will inform school managers how they should perform. In many large districts these administrators are then reduced to passive supervisors of process, presiding over rule systems, meeting unrelenting bureaucratic demands, placating competing constituencies, and avoiding political minefields.

School reform everywhere depends on bold action by local school officials to increase their freedom to cultivate excellence. School boards must endorse scholarship and virtue openly, proudly, and without excuses. In the face of possible community backlash and threat of suits they must have the courage to keep their reforms intact. They might do well, also, to frame an association of sympathetic volunteer lawyers who will, if need be, contribute their services in cases of confrontations, threats, strikes, and suits. While local reformers are building a broad political base, it makes sound strategic sense for them to take a quarrelsome, nonaccommodating, even litigious stance. To try to test their power, they might eliminate trivial courses, dismiss obviously incompetent teachers, or expel suspected student drug dealers. Of all possible barriers to reform, the timidity of discerning district and school officials is the most subversive.

In some urban areas this may be hopeless. Where a top-heavy and multilayered administrative system exists, run by officials who are studiously protecting a hundred job programs, where the union contract is the single standard of teacher responsibility, where pupils' home lives are degraded, and where the courts are eager to make the schools over in the shining image of liberal social doctrine, those who want rapid educational change should probably invest their energies to promote private alternatives. But in most of the nation's sixteen thousand districts conditions are hardly this dire. And even in some sizable districts astonishing improvements can be and have been made.

Take the case of the Modesto, California, school system. It not only provides a clear and replicable model of success for other districts in the country but also shows how far a district can reach in locally based school reform, still "working within the system" and the constraints of its staff, budgets, and structure. Modesto is an agricultural center 90 miles east of San Francisco in the lush San Joaquin Valley. With about twenty thousand students in thirty-one schools, the Modesto system is roughly one-third the size of the Seattle or Pittsburgh systems. Modesto is a fast-growing community, largely nonprofessional, with a substantial Hispanic population and a high number of welfare families. (These are facts that the Modesto system has stopped taking seriously as predictors of student performance.)

In the mid-seventies, as in many other California districts, Modesto's educators faced plunging student achievement. But by 1980 almost 80 percent of the city's students worked at or above grade level in reading and math. On California assessment tests classes scored an average of 10 to 38 percentage points higher in basic skills than in 1976. College-bound students scored on the average about 30 points higher than the SAT verbal national norm. Truancy and serious on-campus discipline problems had all but disappeared.

What did Modesto do? *Nothing magical.* But the system was fortunate to have a relentless, thick-skinned, and supremely sensible assistant superintendent for curriculum and instruction named James

149

C. Enochs. In 1976 Enochs, with the blessing of his board and superintendent, began to revamp the Modesto school system. He did, as a first step, what administrators in most systems consider unthinkable: Enochs acknowledged publicly that Modesto's schools were in serious decline. By documenting local failures, he was able to force many community leaders to acknowledge this fact. He also asserted that Modesto's current policies were likely to exacerbate the decline.

New practices and standards, Enochs and the board agreed, should be installed at once. There were to be no pilot programs, demonstration projects, study committees, "input" and "feedback" hearings, or any other cosmetic reforms designed to slow and minimize their actions. Just as important, they resolved to create a program that would be kept in place for a reasonable amount of time. The board vowed continued support to withstand anticipated waves of criticism.

Enochs introduced the Modesto Plan by announcing new district standards of academic performance and behavior. Henceforth, he said, the district would monitor and publicize how well these goals were met for the district as a whole, for each school, and for every grade level. Then the school board served notice to the local police force, the district attorney's office, the juvenile court, and the mental health and social agencies that the schools were not the only public institutions receiving tax dollars for the purpose of helping children. In the future, it said, the schools would demand more community cooperation and would not act as omnibus welfare organizations. Community leaders were asked to recognize forms of student excellence beyond varsity athletics. Parents were advised of the district's intention to link student rights to responsibilities and, if need be, to expel incorrigible troublemakers. They were reminded of the school's right to dispense differential rewards for outstanding and for mediocre work, as well as to punish corrupt behavior. Restoring the teacher to a position of moral authority was not inherently undemocratic or authoritarian, Enochs and the board declared.

The Modesto Plan's academic program was to encompass grades kindergarten through twelve. Enochs considered it crucial that a regimen with clearly defined expectations touch every grade level. By the time students entered junior high school, where academic and behavioral problems are more grave, he felt students would then be

150

familiar with and accustomed to the competency-based plan. So at every grade level were installed annual assessments of basic skills, including writing from the fourth-grade level on. Students who did not meet the minimum standard would be held back unless their teachers could make a convincing case that the assessment did not reflect the true level of classroom performance.

Upon entering ninth grade, students (and their parents) were to select an academic, vocational, or general course of study, each with its own course requirements. No matter which graduation plan was selected, eleventh-grade students would be required to pass the same battery of tests in reading, writing, mathematics, science, social science, and health. Those who failed any single test would receive remedial help. But any student who did not pass all the tests after two tries would not be graduated from the regular high school program. (He or she could, however, enroll in evening school and qualify for a special diploma.)

The Modesto Plan also included a citizenship program. At the junior and senior high levels each classroom teacher was to assign a quarterly mark, appearing alongside the academic grade, meant to gauge student performance in areas such as being on time, meeting deadlines, bringing materials to class, and completing assignments. If a student received two or more unsatisfactory marks in a single quarter, certain privileges, notably participation in all school-sponsored activities, including sports, would be withheld.

Modesto's academic and citizenship programs were to be tied to active control of truancy. During school hours police officers were instructed to scoop up students loitering on the streets without a legitimate excuse, delivering them to a central location. Parents were then required to pick up their children and take them back to school. If a student was truant eight times, either all day or part of the day, he or she was to be expelled for the rest of the semester. Later parents would have to petition the school for their child's readmission. (Today, by the way, Enochs asserts that in his experience the conventional wisdom that to expel truants is to give them what they want has proved to be a myth. "They plead with us not to expel them, they all petition for readmission, and the marginal truants give it up as a way of life," he says. Enochs also notes that community support for the truancy control plan was tepid—until data showed that the program was accompanied by a significant decline in daytime crime.)

According to Enochs, the implementation of the Modesto Plan proceeded through seven stages, "more phases than the moon," he comments. They should give any quality-minded school board some idea of what to expect in any serious local reform initiative. Phase One was marked by staff cynicism and student disbelief, Enochs says. The dominant local opinion was that the district office would not have the courage to enforce its plan. In Phase Two there was general disregard of the plan by students and parents, followed by unpleasant consequences. (In 1978, the first year the math competency test was administered, 56 percent of the city's ninth-grade students failed it, a figure that decreased to 15 percent for the same students in tenth grade. The following year about twenty athletes in one high school were dismissed from their squad for low citizenship marks, which outraged many Modesto residents.) Phase Three was notable for community panic over the reform plan. Phase Four, almost indistinguishable from Three, Enochs recalls, was marked by anger, vocal calls to scrap the program, charges of programmatic elitism and discrimination, contentious board elections, cries for the assistant superintendent's scalp, and the threat of board retreat.

At this point, Phase Five, Enochs lobbied his board vigorously. He pointed out its early commitment to excellence and its promise to leave the plan in place despite criticism. He reminded it how bad things had been before the reforms had been installed. In Phase Six a quaking and agonized school board reaffirmed the Modesto Plan in a split vote. Staff, students, and the town began to sense the district's resolve and determination. Finally, in Phase Seven student outcomes started to improve dramatically. The board and Enochs became something of local heroes. The Modesto Plan became an article of community pride. (The city's newspaper, for example, now includes a regular weekly column listing outstanding student achievement in speech, art, music, academic competition, student government, attendance, school service, and citizenship.)

The Modesto Plan grew out of a local political coalition that succeeded in increasing district standards and revising school rules during a four-year period. It was effected in the absence of external pressure or guidance, within federal and state guidelines, at no increased district cost and in spite of the local NEA affiliate. In Modesto and elsewhere, more extensive reform is theoretically possible, though it would be a great advance in the coming decade if thousands of districts simply came close to adopting the city's standards.

The Modesto case confirms the possibility of far-reaching reform when a kernel of the community desires it. Yet constraints on educational change are formidable. In Modesto and elsewhere, educators who press for alterations in public school operations repeatedly run into inert and hostile colleagues, often backed up by interest groups and modern social theories. On several sensitive fronts even slight adjustments, when proposed, provoke stricken outbursts among people who are threatened by them or who misperceive what is educationally good for children. We should look at four of these areas, at once acknowledging internal barriers to reform and presenting possible ways to surmount them.

EDUCATIONAL FINANCE AND VALUE

This will remain politically difficult: to contend that reducing some educational budget lines will have a beneficial impact on schools; that even in underfinanced cities financial problems grow as much out of misallocations as shortages; and that in coming years those who want better schools must stop equating education dollars spent with the quality of educational delivery.

School reformers must pay new attention to value received per dollar. To their advantage amelioration does not require greater infusions of public money, as long as deficient personnel and programs are being phased out and the savings are being transferred to productive ends. To their disadvantage the fierce collective power of those who cavort in federal- and state-based funds may crush any such initiatives.

To see how well-intentioned money sometimes comes to no good ends, consider the past experience of one district with the former Emergency School Assistance Act (ESAA). Authorized by Congress

153

after 1971 to reduce busing tensions and "encourage the voluntary elimination, reduction, and prevention of minority group isolation in elementary and secondary schools," ESAA was in 1979 the seventh largest category of federal education aid. (The largest comprised programs for the educationally deprived, notably Title I, funded at about $3 billion, or ten times the size of ESAA.) The stated ends of ESAA were noble, but what were the *means* toward these ends?

For the district in question, in 1981, ESAA money opened up scores of special jobs for project heads, academic support teachers, parent leadership specialists, student activities specialists, outreach/intervention counselors, outreach/counseling aides, counseling team leaders, and program evaluators. Each of the city's dozen or so high schools was given about $6,000 to spend on student game rooms, field trips, and assemblies, all with the intention of improving dismal race relations among students. In one high school this was more than the *entire* athletic budget. The dean unwillingly put in charge of the program said, "The federal government is telling us how to waste money."

ESAA was not the most ineffectual or objectionable old reform initiative in force in schools. But this is precisely the point. Like other authorizations spun from Great Society instrumentalism, it siphoned away funds for capital maintenance and improvement, janitorial and security services, and academic instruction. To put it differently, it diverted funds that could pay for effective teaching and attractive campuses. Resources went instead toward funding make-work jobs, creating self-perpetuating networks with webbed interest in sustaining programs. And any reformer attempting to modify or extinguish these networks could prepare to be called educationally insensitive or worse.

SCHOOL STRUCTURE AND POPULATIONS

Many new school reformers are now constructing elaborate fantasies of increased school diversity, especially at the secondary level. They might think again. The harsh fact is that in most localities the all-purpose, large-scale secondary school is here to stay. Critics rightly liken these huge educational plants in ambience to factories and shopping malls. But most of these schools are too entrenched in their communities to be deconsolidated; they are too efficient in terms of fixed and variable costs; they centralize too many different social services. And quite literally by design, such schools do not lend themselves to internal conversion.

Through the century most American adolescents will be schooled in large-scale settings. This is unfortunate. Arguably, small secondary schools are more conducive to high educational outcomes than cost-effective comprehensive schools. Small secondary schools, that is, schools with student populations ranging between several hundred and one thousand, seem to make up for their alleged resource deficiencies by achieving higher levels of school solidarity and purpose. Administrations tend to be more concentrated and less intimidating. Introverted and alienated students are less invisible and anonymous; they are more likely to be forced into regular interactions with adults. In small schools, too, each student has a greater opportunity to find an extracurricular niche from which to exercise some authority or earn some sort of schoolwide reputation and trademark.

In coming years districts that have enough money and vacant plant to do so should make efforts to create small schools or to subdivide large schools. But many more districts will be forced to rely on comprehensive schools. These structural constraints make it all the more important to establish climates where institutional impersonality does not give rise to apathy or belligerence. They make it all the more important for students to conform and adjust to a purposeful academic or vocational program. To encourage such atmospheres, and to protect the welfare of the majority, minimally committed, disturbed, and delinquent children must be excluded from regular secondary programs—and not after countless reprimands or full-blown court reviews.

The problem, then, is what to do with dropouts, expellees, and other displaced teenagers. They certainly do not belong in school. But then where? Alternative and evening schools offer one solution. But the new school reformers may encounter an unexpected cultural dilemma: Some neurasthenic, antisocial, and dangerous children probably require constructive therapeutic treatment that our society cannot bear to give them. To learn to discipline themselves, work hard, conform to laws, and abide by community standards, some young people may require special quasi-educational facilities that would borrow from the models of the Civilian Conservation Corps, Outward Bound, or Marine boot camp.

Yet a permissive society probably finds it too disagreeable and authoritarian to subject children to harsh sanctions. Unconsciously it may be less taxing to recognize, so to speak, rights of anomie. The will of the republic seems to prefer juvenile rebelliousness, drug addiction, criminal activity, and welfare dependency to what some might call "cruel and unusual" discipline. If public secondary schools are to thrive, they cannot be obliged to make room for every youth, including those whose problems are the proper domain of the police and hospitals. But as yet in our communities and courts, a toxic romanticism prevents needed treatments and reforms.

Course Content

In coming years empowering academic content and imposing new course requirements may be the reform activities most likely to generate rapid school improvements. Curriculum alteration is not only relatively cost-free. Already heralded course innovations of the sixties and seventies have become a macabre national joke. Wisely the courts have shied away from entering the curriculum business. And agreeable trends are apparent.

In all but the most degraded schools and districts there is new interest in promoting the structure and forms of standard English. District administrators and government officials are genuinely worried by the unspeakable condition of mathematical and scientific training at the secondary level. Former champions of vocational education including the Chamber of Commerce are now emphasizing cognitive skills and abstract reasoning powers that entry-level workers need for on-the-job training in the skilled and technical trades.

Career education and work–study programs have not provided, as promised, a favorable interactive structure between adults and adolescents, nor have they cured juvenile alienation, taught industry and discipline, or elevated the status of manual labor. Instead, it seems that work–study students tend to withdraw emotionally from school and grow academically unmotivated. By earning a modest income at the expense of academic skills, the same students may delude themselves that they are "ahead of the game." But they stay in front only a short time, since they usually lack the mental powers to handle jobs much above the minimum wage level. Those favoring career education claim that it provides needed skills to bridge the world of intellect and the world of work. Arthur E. Wise responds: "No skills have been so identified, unless one considers them to be associated with liberal education."

In ten years or so we might hope that the vast majority of high school graduates will complete an academic program, being able to write a logical and mechanically correct five-page expository paper, to solve for an algebraic unknown, and to explain how a bill becomes a law. For students with developed vocational interests we might hope that such academic competencies would apply, although with more elective emphasis on the applied uses of academic knowledge and the possibility of early admission into community and technical colleges. We might hope that curriculum specialists will support initiatives to reintroduce practices such as final examinations and required remedial summer sessions.

But how far can academic reform reach? Several obstacles stand out. Ongoing intrafaculty suspicions and turf battles will tend to inhibit coherent curricular planning. No realistic reforms can take place when many high school instructors must direct the learning of 120 or more restless pupils each day and are supposed to be available for discussions, committees, counseling sessions, and extracurricular assignments before retiring at the end of the day to grade homework, the education researcher Theodore R. Sizer has correctly remarked. Faculty members who are lazy or intellectually weak will do everything in their power to obstruct more rigorous course content and teaching methods. In schools where a psychology of defeatism prevails, adults will not have sufficient self-confidence to make children work to their potential. Is it realistic for the new reformers to argue for a required high school course in computer science, replacing courses in health education, on the grounds that health can be learned outside the classroom but

157

that every young citizen must know something about data storage and processing? Is it possible to argue for a required yearlong course in Latin, one that stresses a systematic grammar, etymological foundations, and the ancient matrix of European civilization?

In curriculum reform, especially in the social studies, we also run against competing cultural ideologies. How committed are educators and their leaders to teaching children about the external world? Do they treat the images of places, events, traditions, laws, and mores that bind children to community with reverence? Do they convey resentment of those images? Or do they share with their students the suspicion that what matters most is the development of "awareness" and subjective feelings in each individual's private cosmos?

Teacher Quality and Incentives

Education depends on the people charged with the formal duty to instruct the young. And every school reformer should cringe at the sorry spectacle of the beleaguered, unappreciated, underpaid, and badly managed American teacher, a reform obstacle of enormous proportions.

In the calculus of student outcomes, the factors of government mandates, competency objectives, family disposition, and so much more play crucial roles. But the instant the classroom door is shut, these forces are driven toward the margin. It is the teacher, no one else, who *engages* pupils in the dynamic act of learning. For good or ill the teacher becomes the authoritative intermediary between each student and some technique, process, created thing, or event.

Along the margin salutary structural and administrative changes might occur. The rhetoric of academic excellence might rush forth in dazzling cascades. Yet without an adequate, and constantly replenished, stock of sound, dedicated, and reasonably intelligent practitioners, school improvement is likely to elude reformers. Perhaps for this reason, then, Sizer has said, "Teacher quality might be the Achilles' heel of school improvement in the eighties." Stanford's education dean, J. Myron Atkin, adds: "There is the somewhat chilling possibility that the schools today may be staffed as well as they will be for the next decade."

Sizer's and Atkin's pessimism may be based on their full understanding of multiple obstacles in teacher recruitment and retention. Any reformers interested in offering new inducements to capable prospective teachers and new rewards to superior veterans will collide with equity-minded associations. They will encounter university education departments and state licensing agencies intent on protecting certification monopolies at the risk of excluding accomplished scholars. They will face district procedures that would grant tenure to an Aurelius or a Caligula after three years and later advance Caligula at the same salary schedule as Aurelius. They will run up against the personnel dictates of the federal courts, and perhaps not only in hiring. Last year a Boston appeals court put a new wrinkle in schoolhouse affirmative action: It ruled that staff *reductions* in the troubled Boston system were to take place not on the basis of seniority (as stipulated by contract) but on the basis of race (to protect minority jobs and racial balance). As a result the court affirmed an order discharging more than six hundred white teachers with an average of ten years' seniority, even as new black teachers were being hired.

What has been the central goal of concerted teacher organization during the last generation? For unionists in both the NEA and the AFT, the stated goal has been increased financial benefits, legal protection, and job security for all. In contrast to the AFT's policies, the NEA's dominant official outlook seems hostile toward the nation's past and present record and apathetic toward strict standards of character. Yet by shielding the lazy and inept along with the gifted, either organization's union card has acted as a powerful disincentive to teacher productivity and initiative. The AFT especially once stressed the historical exploitation and oppression of teachers, deriding the service ethic. Not unexpectedly, the vocational aspect of teaching, with its pastoral authority, discretionary power, and likelihood of community veneration, has atrophied, to be replaced by a contract and a legal defense fund. We are a long way from Dewey, who at the turn of the century talked of the teacher as "the usherer in of the true kingdom of God."

159

As some union leaders would have it, the declining attractiveness of teaching for people of sensitivity and ability is a simple function of salary. Pay teachers more, they say, and quality problems will disappear. Few school observers doubt that *good* teachers are grossly underpaid. But the dominant trade union position, which advocates increased and indiscriminate compensation for *all* teachers, is more aligned to group self-interest than to school improvement.

What dogmatic unionists have lost sight of or not understood is that for many instructors, and most of the best, the appeal of teaching rests in the satisfaction derived from the job. Such teachers enter the classroom anticipating more pleasure than financial reward. If this psychic income is withheld or on the wane, teachers are likely to seek other careers or decline in productivity. And while psychic income remains high for many individual teachers, it is dropping for teachers as a group. The prevailing sense that schools have limited effect on the general welfare cuts at teachers' self-worth. Procedural guidelines, assorted regulations, and legal manacles discourage teachers of independent character who desire considerable discretionary power. "The skepticism toward those in responsible positions and the erosion of civility within the community have been reflected faithfully among children," Atkin has commented. He might have added that many people considering a career will reconcile themselves to the possibility of some friction and rudeness among adult co-workers; these same people refuse to be objects of abuse by children. Alarmingly, about 40 percent of all teachers—twice as many as ten years ago—now say that they regret their decision to become teachers. Sixty-eight percent of all adult Americans consider teaching an unattractive job for young people, according to a 1981 Gallup Poll.

College students know which way the wind blows. Between 1974 and 1981 the proportion of college students considering teaching careers fell from 23 to 6 percent. During the last ten years teacher production has declined by half, and in key areas, such as mathematics and science, the applicant pool for teacher training may be falling toward zero. Worse, the most able pool of prospective teachers has dried up: No longer are the avenues into medicine, law, and business blocked to bright female and nonwhite students. Not surprisingly, such individuals seek more lucrative, prestigious, satisfying jobs. According to a 1979 report by W. Timothy Weaver, a Boston University education professor, college-bound seniors planning to become teachers and taking the SAT in 1976 scored on average 34 points below the national norm on the verbal section and 43 points below on the mathematics section.* During the seventies the intellectual ability of teachers as measured by the Graduate Record and National Teacher examinations declined. In tested academic talent, Weaver concluded, new teachers ranked very near the bottom of the white-collar occupations.

Those intent on improving public schools should have no illusions about their competition and, in fact, could learn from them. Private schools, which pay lower teacher salaries, draw on an average more academically accomplished university graduates than public schools. These private school faculties, officially uncertified and unqualified, also have higher occupational status and produce better average student outcomes. Teachers work in private schools in part because they accurately sense greater institutional respect for their qualities of mind and individuality. They can demand respect from their clients, expecting parents and children to be polite to them. They can exercise powers *in loco parentis* more comfortably and gain the satisfactions this entails. They do not abide time clocks and generally have control over their own syllabuses. In return they are generally expected to hold an explicit service ethic, to act as partners in the regulation of standards, and to dress as respectably as a country lawyer or banker. These are professional rewards and responsibilities, as everyone should know, and to obtain them private school teachers relinquish some job security and income.

School reformers in the eighties must make more efforts to retain and reward veteran instructors who have a sense of mission, special talents, or original and profound minds. Just as important, they must recruit enough young replacements to offset rising attrition and early retirements. To do this, education leaders might consider some of

---

* By 1980 the respective figures were 35 and 48. According to another compilation, in 1979 high school seniors planning to become education majors averaged 392 on their SAT verbal, compared with 505 for those planning to major in English, 498 for those planning to major in the physical sciences, and 476 for those planning to major in library science.

161

the following avenues to stimulate professionalism and instructional excellence:

- *Outside Review of Teacher-training Programs.* State governments should urge university officials to convene blue-ribbon panels of academic professors to review courses of study leading to teacher certification. Such panels should be empowered by their institutions or states to mandate, when necessary, strict guidelines for education-school overhaul.
- *Increased Degree Options.* Undergraduates should not be forced to choose between intellectual pursuits and certification. Certification programs might be moved to the domain of liberal arts committees, which can install a required education major grounded in composition and literature, history and philosophy, mathematics and computer science, foreign language, and natural science. But liberal arts majors and those holding advanced degrees in the humanities and sciences should also be able to qualify for certification. All "special" education courses should be pushed to the graduate level and not be necessary preconditions to academic teaching.
- *More Flexible Retention Systems.* School executives, especially principals, need greater autonomy in staffing. In a time of declining enrollments and budget squeezes, thousands of districts must cut back on personnel. How can marginally useful or able staff be pared, though, when reductions-in-force are decided on seniority or on race? Administrators should be granted the means to advise out, force into early retirement, or dismiss obviously ignorant, contentious, slovenly, and odd teachers of any age. Granted, superintendents, principals, and department heads are not always omniscient or even fair, but excessive contractual protections check attempts to make reasonable judgments about individual teachers or, more precisely, to make staff cutbacks based on these judgments.
- *Limited Tenure.* Formerly, teacher tenure was a needed protection against authoritarian administrators and crabbed community standards. Today it is an obstacle to school improvement. A half-century of extended civil rights protections has rendered

162

the original purpose of tenure codes obsolete. These protections, however, remain on the books, proof of statehouse inability to stem the privileges gained by union-based political action groups. In dealing with marginal staff, perhaps, school officials should try to honor the claims of seniority and the virtue of charity. Rules must be relaxed so that administrators can dispatch tenured teachers for acts short of selling liquor to students or embezzling school funds. For teachers, tenure should be seen as an authentic grant-in-merit instead of a near-right.

- *Open Salary and Title Differentiation.* In such fields as mathematics, science, and vocational education, where teacher shortages already exist, school boards need to construct salary schedules higher than in other fields, such as English or social studies, where teacher surpluses exist. Districts should also advance teachers in stages, perhaps from intern to associate instructor (an untenured position that could be held as short as three years but as long as twenty) to tenured instructor to senior (or master) teacher. Each progressive stage should offer substantially higher salary schedules and make other special merit rewards.
- *More Parity Between Administrative and Teaching Salaries.* No educator, including district officials and principals, should have strong pecuniary interest in leaving and remaining outside the classroom. School boards should set pay schedules so that it is equally (or more) rewarding to be a senior teacher as, say, an athletic director or dean of discipline.
- *Added Teacher Perquisites.* General funds should make money available to districts so that all localities can establish ample sabbatical plans, mortgage assistance programs, competitions for summer study, early retirement plans, and more. University education and academic departments should throw out more cables to their natural allies, recruiting senior teachers as adjunct faculty and associates.
- *Leadership.* Assistant principals become principals, principals are shuffled around, principals become assistant superintendents, and assistant superintendents become superintendents— in other school systems. According to one estimate, the average

163

tenure of a district superintendent is between three and five years. With such enormous administrative discontinuity, many teachers—educators who do not move from job to job and place to place—have learned that nothing is certain but change. They have grown cynical about reform plans that are revised on an annual basis. They, too, rarely have the stable leadership whose first concerns are faculty standards, morale, dignity, and pride.

It would be a splendid dream if teaching masters could mobilize their unions and colleagues toward such ends. But this possibility seems remote because, as Dan C. Lortie, a University of Chicago sociologist, and others say, gifted teachers exist usually by dint of highly personal and idiosyncratic methods, individual charisma, a private love of learning, and the inner happiness derived from at once working for and commanding the young. Most master teachers probably desire most that the bureaucratic apparatus of their school leave them alone so that they may pursue their own unconventional ends.

~~~~~~~

In school reform there are faint and encouraging signs of change. There is not yet cause for trumpets. Many educators, nonetheless, seeing slight ticks upward after precipitous declines, are already proclaiming that and saying the bad times over and saying that all is well again. This is especially so in the case of SAT scores. These are the same school leaders whose speeches and articles now begin, "To be sure, academic learning is the central aim of schools . . . " then somersault into making a case for another new mission or scheme. Either deluded or cynical, these leaders conceive the most superficial changes in program to be monumental. They want trumpets but few adjustments. In coming years marginal changes posing as dramatic turnarounds and initiatives may be the most insidious and granitelike barriers to still fragile qualitative reform efforts.

TEN

The Cultivation
of Excellence

In EDUCATIONAL CIRCLES TODAY the buzzword is excellence. How to create more effective schools is the issue at hand, and none too soon in schools where little learning takes place and where chaos prevails. Yet some of those now climbing onto the quality bandwagon give every impression that they are acting more out of expediency than out of conviction. Still more refuse to endorse salutary practices that they have long claimed to be elitist, discriminatory, or overly rigorous. Like Harvard's late Stephen K. Bailey, writing in *Daedalus*, they sniff that "current rhetoric about the alleged failure of schooling is simply the most recent incarnation of a tired and sullen litany."

Not exactly. Some of the freshest impulses in school reform, no doubt, could have been cribbed from the essays of Bagley and Bestor. But through what we know from new research and studies, these older Essentialists had a sounder idea of what makes schools work than many of their Progressive contemporaries and reforming successors. Critics like Bailey seem disconcerted that for almost five decades, in spite of the zigs and zags of educational novelty, Essentialists have espoused the cause of excellence. And these critics have reason to

165

be worried that the very theories and precepts they have long deplored may be the sine qua non of educational recovery. Today it is the political and philosophical legacy of the sixties that sounds tired and sullen, not to say destitute of program.

This is not to denigrate all recent Progressive achievements. Before the end of the third quarter of the century, equity-driven reformers orchestrated and realized a series of thoroughgoing changes in U.S. schooling. To young people formerly ignored or discriminated against, they gave access to education. They forced educators to become even more sensitive to individual instructional needs. To aid disadvantaged youngsters, they expanded school welfare services. They spent many billions of dollars to underwrite important research, improve educational materials, and create a sturdy national education plant. They assisted teachers in efforts to organize and gain contractually protected benefits once undreamed of.

Yet there was one fatal flaw. Few sixties- and seventies-style reformers were very interested in protecting and advancing high standards of scholarship or discipline. They lost sight of the school's communal, conserving obligations to sustain what is best in the civilization. Once in control of the education establishment, they let their salient interests in cultural pluralism, group compensation, and subject novelties render them blind to falling student outcomes. Through the seventies new ideas and initiatives that seemed to them wise, penetrating, shrewd, and politic struck more and more of their clients as muddled, silly, and finally offensive. Gradually the liberal consensus's view came to seem implausible.

Renewed interest in scholastic quality comes at the very moment that elementary and secondary education enter, willy-nilly, an epoch of profound strain. Declining enrollments and budgetary constraints may force thousands of school districts to decrease services and eliminate programs, to lay off teachers and other school workers, to cut tissue with the fat. This crunch could well result in trench warfare among special interest groups, pinchpenny drives to dismantle important school services in the name of "economy," and worse.

But the coming era of retrenchment could also be a time of great opportunities, when schools can reconsider which of their functions

166

are most necessary. Counterproductive, badly implemented, or too-costly activities can be modified and streamlined. Bankrupt methods and incompetent personnel might be removed altogether. The proper debate of the eighties should be over how to contract on behalf of quality—in other words, how to get rid of peripheral activities, un-needed staff, and worn-out ideas with an eye toward increasing out-comes and productivity.

Given the current climate of elementary and secondary reform, principles of traditional schooling need review. As a foundation for more effective schools of tomorrow, let us consider the following pre-cepts of schooling.

All students should receive instruction in academic subjects and thereby have the opportunity to develop their intellectual abilities to the fullest extent possible. What some call basic education considers the transmis-sion of general knowledge schooling's primary and unique cultural function. The content of the liberal arts and sciences must be *every* school's "first curriculum." For if academic subjects and skills are not learned in school, then where *will* they be learned? By teaching young people to read and more, schools are bound to make a better society. Why must schools also try to succeed as ersatz families, hospi-tals, and detention centers? First and foremost schools are social agen-cies of intellectual training.

The sociologist Daniel Bell offers one cogent explanation for basic education's preoccupation with the study of language, mathematics, science, history, social studies, and the arts in *The Cultural Contradic-tions of Capitalism.* Such traditional learning "is essential to the vitality of the culture, for it provides the continuity of memory that teaches how one's forebears met the same existential predicaments," he says. The liberal subjects, by this line of reasoning, can "liberate" each new generation. They emancipate each generation from the transitory, incidental, immediate, and insignificant.

Certainly schools can only publish, teach, and test a curriculum. The "learned" curriculum ultimately depends on parents, television, peer groups, and much more. But schools can focus on their honorable role to perpetuate the language, clarify the methods of logic and calcu-

167

lation, explore natural history, inform the young about the origins and possibilities of the present, and in all of this touch on the substance of character.

Put it a different way. Schools have neither the time nor the resources to convey all knowledge. Basic skills permit people to read instructions, listen to directions, assess value and validity, imitate by observation, understand the political and natural laws by which they live, and so on. The content of the basic subjects gives learners the mental equipment to adjust to new situations, tackle the unknown with some confidence, and solve problems efficiently. These are the necessary tools for alert citizens and self-reliant workers. All young people are capable of understanding these subjects. In a working democracy, they all need to.

Almost thirty years ago the literary critic Clifton Fadiman defended what he called the *generative subjects.* "Basic education concerns itself with those matters which, once learned, enable the student to learn all the other matters, whether trivial or complex, that cannot properly be the subjects of elementary and secondary schooling," he said. Robert M. Hutchins wrote, about the same time and in the same vein, "Even if driving a car, understanding plumbing, and behaving like a mature woman are valuable subjects, they can be, and therefore should be, learned outside the educational system."

The basic subjects may not be immediately useful to an eight- or sixteen-year-old in the ways fire safety, community service, sex education, or work experience are "useful." But thought, criticism, reflection, appreciation, comprehension, and achieving one's human potential first require access to the tools and substance of understanding. Deprived of them, an individual becomes at best limited. At worst, he or she is untrainable, hurt, envious, and utterly bewildered by everyday complexities.

General and basic education to what practical purpose? The goals are hardly elitist. As the philosopher Steven M. Cahn says in *Education and the Democratic Ideal,* knowledge is essential if all citizens have the ability, for good or bad, to determine the course of the polity:

> This power of the people presents democracy with its most crucial problem, for what defense is there against a narrow-minded or

gullible citizenry? If the public cannot distinguish reason from demagogy, integrity from duplicity, wisdom from folly, then all is lost. For not only is an open society susceptible to a misguided majority, but by its very nature it offers avenues to power for potential tyrants who, having availed themselves of freedom, would at the first opportunity deny it to others.

So the crucial question is: How can the members of a democracy be provided with the necessary understanding and capability to reap the greatest possible benefits from the democratic process while at the same time protecting that process from those who would seek its destruction? The answer is to be found in the enterprise of education.

Now it becomes clear why in a democracy every individual's education should be of such vital concern. For the ignorance of some is a threat to all.

Students do not progress at the same pace when learning the academic subjects. Even a single pupil's facility with different subjects and topics may vary: the math whiz who cannot spell, for example, or the child who can recite all the state capitals but cannot understand that climates vary in different regions of the world. Some students are smarter, more ambitious, or more diligent than others. Yet these facts should not be construed to mean that an academic education should apply only to the most gifted and hardest-working.

The impossibility of equal attainments cannot deter schools from offering equal opportunities of academic access. Schools must equally serve the bright, the average, and the slow pupil, even though individual students are destined to progress at different speeds. And they serve the least able and the minimally committed best when such students are traveling the road of the fundamental disciplines, albeit less quickly and less far. The ideal of formal education for all students, of course, should not be minimum but maximum competency.

In light of the miserably low standards set in recent years for less able and minority youngsters, it is valuable to recall what Arthur Bestor wrote long ago in *The Restoration of Learning:*

> In extending educational opportunity, however, we are honor-bound not to lower its quality, for if we do we are defrauding the common man of the very intellectual and cultural privileges we have promised, at long last, to open up to him. . . . An educa-

tional philosophy is both anti-intellectual and anti-democratic if it asserts that sound training in the fundamental intellectual disciplines is appropriate only for the minority of students who are preparing for college and the professions, and if it proposes to deprive the rest of the children of our people of such training by substituting programs that minimize intellectual aims.

All courses of study and teaching methods should be subjected to rigorous critical examination to determine whether they promote intellect and self-discipline. Objectionable school practices usually stem from excessive faith in the value of novelty or impatience and apathy toward general knowledge. They come from uncertainty over the steering responsibilities of adults and the desire to make learning above all fun. Foolish curricular revisions, lax teaching methods, and grandiose social programs in force throughout the country are the bitter fruit of quick-fix "humanizing" correctives proposed and sometimes adopted by those neutral toward or contemptuous of traditional subjects and values.

Educators should welcome and encourage changes in curricula and methods, of course, and need to now that so many recent innovations in both these areas have crippled school operations. Henceforth, needed revisions in syllabuses and lesson plans, in campus rules, in programs for troubled or disadvantaged youngsters, and in the theoretical frameworks of schooling should be tested on the basis of whether or not each assists or hinders performance. Change should be based on what the record shows to promote the content and skills of the basic academic subjects and what creates disciplined students, not on what at any moment seems exciting and topical.

There is urgent need for accessible and dispassionate critical studies of past and projected innovations, both what they aim to accomplish and how well they achieve their ends. Many of the schoolhouse catastrophes of our times have achieved customary status out of district-level follow-the-leaderism and unsound program evaluation. And many unproductive programs remain, sustained by organized loathing of quality control in most educational trade associations and by inept, biased, or contradictory research.

Educational researchers in the eighties must try to answer some hard questions. Why, for example, is the positive academic impact of so many major federal and state educational initiatives still unproved? Why do research studies of these programs exhibit incredible variations in their conclusions? Why do patently ineffective programs remain in place? Why, for all the billions of dollars that governments, foundations, and universities have poured into the study of schooling, do we know so little about entire aspects of the educational enterprise, for instance, the impact of the student rights revolution, the causes of teacher attrition, the status of the civics curriculum, or the needs of average children?

Clear standards of performance should be set for all students, and those standards should govern the rate of student advancement. In many schools student underachievement and even nonachievement have become an unofficial right. At present most pupils who are graduated from public high schools with satisfactory levels of achievement must supply their own standards, come from families that hold high expectations for them, be guided into demanding courses where teachers drive them to produce, or be seeking admission to selective colleges. The high school diploma is not a reliable and universal certificate of academic mastery.

Too many children face school situations in which educators cannot come near consensus on school aims and requirements. Too many teachers mark solely on the basis of effort or good behavior, ignore test results, or have difficulty discerning superior and inferior work. In many schools students may be advanced—socially promoted—rewarded, and simultaneously deprived of the foundations they need to compete at higher levels of learning. By the junior or senior high school level, where course content is more complicated and abstract, some pupils may be so deficient in the basic skills that their fellow classmates might be held back by the remedial needs of a few. In some secondary schools, where stated grade levels have lost all meaning, course content simply ceases to advance in complexity—a system which punishes, cheats, and injures every attending student.

Examination and grading systems ranking individual accomplishment—including failure—assure a standard of minimum achievement for all pupils. At every grade level schools should publish and enforce

171

well-defined exit criteria that are more advanced than entrance criteria. Ideally, all but a few fifth graders should understand the single-digit multiplication table, all eighth graders should have some control over commas and fractions, and all high school diplomas should stand for literacy that is more than inert.

But when students fail classroom exercises or register low scores on standardized tests, educators should under no circumstances assume that poor outcomes are necessarily the fault of the students, the grading system, or the examining tools. Unsatisfactory academic results often signal a need for substantial changes in instructional methods or in curricular content.

How far can these changes go? Trying to create well-defined and rigorous standards by which educators can measure student merit presents two intractable problems. First, making distinctions of any kind is likely to arouse the suspicion and anxiety of those who believe that their own interests will be jeopardized by the resulting standard. In a relativistic age standard-setting rarely occurs without complaints from individuals that guidelines are arbitrary or brutalizing. Many minority groups try to make the point that color-blind standards are discriminatory. Chagrined by inequalities and intimidated by pressure groups, many education leaders find it personally or politically impossible to install standards designed to make every individual try his best to achieve value or excellence against impartial or at least normative models. In the classroom many teachers resist gauging inadequate, average, and superior performances, a concept that the same educators will recognize, accept, and endorse in various school sports and extra-curricular activities.

A second constraint on proper evaluation is a large number of educators stuck in the mire of low expectations for themselves, their students, and their schools. They support mediocrity because it has become their own taste, standard, and norm. As Portland, Maine, school superintendent Peter R. Greer has asserted gloomily, many adults in schools cannot even recognize models of excellence. And in such cases, he says, when high standards are articulated and introduced, these educators are incapable of implementing them. Stated district standards that are estimable then become meaningless in day-to-day school operations. Correcting this depends on the increased ability of districts to hire people of intellect, good judgment, and taste and to dismiss those who have none of these traits.

Educators should hold high expectations for students of all backgrounds and capabilities. Adults in schools can require young people to work as hard and behave as virtuously as themselves. Assuming that educators are reasonably hardworking and decent, they can even abide by a frank "double standard," seeing their enforced standard for children as an ideal standard or *ought* for themselves. Schools can emphasize the self-respect derived from genuine accomplishment, from hard and sustained work, from familiarity with high culture, from overcoming what at first seem to be insurmountable obstacles. Such standards seem particularly important for low-achieving and nonwhite students, often lulled into inactivity by teachers and counselors who feel that "special needs" should take precedence over learning or who are secretly convinced that students' backgrounds render them incapable of equaling the teachers' own accomplishments. This is therapeutic, caring discrimination, really the latest chapter in the long and debilitating history of life-adjustment education, a continuing pestilence of our times.

What is important for the society at large is irrelevant or impossible for these sad and disadvantaged children, this line of reasoning goes. Never quite articulated, an ethos of low expectations dominates some schools, coming from many directions: from teachers, who spend only a few minutes each hour actually working on lessons; from curriculum specialists, who say that reading has little meaning for children from desolate homes; from textbook publishers, who develop comic book texts and "television-competitive" materials; from activities directors, who prefer disco dances to formal assemblies; and from education professors, who assert that minority dialects are on a par with standard English forms. So much of what is "caring" in education today is in fact insulting, condescending, and vulgar.

In school improvement, of course, character must count. The pursuit of excellence requires all students to learn very early that school is a special place, where gratification must sometimes be deferred, where certain classroom topics are more important than one's immediate interests and are too grave to be amusing. Schools must be places where all students are obliged to exhibit a reasonable threshold of frustration and a modicum of effort, in other words, a rudimentary work ethic. Schools must be orderly and, one should hope, spirited, friendly places. Young people who are actively alienated by all available curricula or who are disruptive and threatening must learn that they can lose their "right" to go to school. And adults in schools must have sufficient sanctions to enforce high classroom and campus standards, thereby protecting themselves, their students, school property, and the climate of learning.

The ethos of striving is contagious. The key is recognition and the satisfaction of doing something well. Honor rolls and societies, plays and recitals, baking and science fairs, spelling bees, intramural athletic events, and essay prizes can do wonders for dispirited schools. Youngsters—if not all their faint-hearted elders—seem to enjoy low-risk competition. Young people benefit from meeting a standard and being rewarded for some task that they have completed well.

School personnel should be competent by education, training, and temperament to carry out their assigned responsibilities. For too long qualitative reformers have called for improved teacher education, not a bad aim but one that ignores less visible adults in schools. Superintendents, district officials, principals, deans, aides, and support staff need public scrutiny as well. All who derive their office or salaries from the educational enterprise have a civic trust in their disposition toward excellence.

The cultivation of excellence first requires educators unwilling to shelter the least able in their profession. It then requires educators who take on faith that most good teaching pressures and directs students, who accept a conditional morality not emphasizing rebelliousness or self-assertion for themselves or children, who think that the content of general knowledge takes precedence over a teacher's or a child's topical interests. It finally requires educators who make it clear to all that their standards of excellence are not mere expressions of personal preferences but necessary definitions of knowledge attained.

Not every adult is suited to work in schools, especially not those who for some reason or other are hostile toward academic learning. No educator at any level has the individual right to oppose the concept of a "first curriculum," that is, the existence of a sound academic program taking precedence over all other realms of school life. No educator at any level has the right to put the noneducational activities of schools ahead of the "first curriculum." Only after given a firm commitment to the school as the nursery of intellect should a school community turn its attention to new pastoral and nonacademic tasks.

One might suppose that in an era of reductions-in-force personnel improvement would be simple. Get rid of poor administrators and teachers, then hire better ones, lay people often say. If only that were possible! Staff reform encounters many obstacles: seniority rules, tenure laws, affirmative-action programs, a monopoly system of teacher certification, low and inflexible pay scales, the declining attractiveness of school jobs, the declining intellectual ability of those who want them. While such systemic rigidities may be adjusted in coming years—and should be—none is likely to vanish. Yet localities can do much, as Superintendent Greer has declared. Citizens can first elect capable school committee members who will in large part determine the quality of the school system, setting sound directions for the district and hiring a tough-minded superintendent. That superintendent must be willing to carry out those instructions, stand up to the local union affiliates, manage the central office staff, and convey his or her interest in high student outcomes to all the district's principals.

School principals, for their part, must be willing to take corrective action with mediocre or hopeless teachers, including not renewing contracts and dismissing the do-nothings. It is the school principal, as the education scholar Chester E. Finn, Jr., has said, who is the institution's "chief protector of educational internalities." That is, the principal more than anyone else at the building level will determine the overall level of school effectiveness. The principal can resist interferences with the "first curriculum," establish and maintain high standards, steer the faculty toward self-improvement, introduce new techniques that promote student achievement, and try to procure the ablest possible staff.

But unfortunately, Finn admits,

Too many principals are former teachers or coaches whose only formal preparation for an executive role were some cook-book courses offered by the school administration department of the local teachers' college. Too many principals are people whose foremost value is not rocking the boat; others may once have tried to rock it but gave up when they were rebuked by their superiors, undercut by their subordinates, or defeated by the avalanche of often conflicting tasks imposed on them by outside forces, including state or federal governments.

Like their curriculum directors and department heads, principals need organized courses of study to learn more about law and public policy, school finances, and recent research on effective schooling, a kind of training that few graduate schools of education yet offer. And the *best* principals continue to teach at least one part of a course. Unless they are in constant touch with the classroom, principals sink to the base level of passive managers.

Teaching, severed from a sense of vocation, becomes a desultory and frustrating way to make a living. School instructors need constant reminders—and not through bumper-sticker campaigns or occasional testimonial dinners—that what they do is important. Any board, superintendent, or principal unable to generate teacher *esprit* will face inferior schools. Teachers, for their part, must be sensitive to their responsibilities beyond the union contract. They cannot delude themselves that a legal agreement contains, somewhere in the fine print, their every obligation. They cannot shield their incompetent colleagues. As communicators of knowledge to an unlettered generation, they must understand that what they do—often without proper recognition or remuneration—can help to advance or harm the society's quality of life.

The school's support staff—secretaries, cafeteria workers, bus drivers, janitors, and security guards—comprises the least appreciated group of school adults. Yet young people spend time in their company during a large part of the day. By temperament, such workers should be civil, wholesome, and forgiving. Conversely, they must *never* be subjected to danger or insult in the places where they work. A knife-wielding youth in a school cafeteria is a far more immediate threat to a lunchroom aide than he is to a district judge worrying about juvenile procedural rights.

176

Educators should resist efforts to increase school responsibility for the social and psychological welfare of students. The Progressive Century's signal triumph has been near-universal recognition that school aims should extend beyond the creation of a literate population. Noneducational services in schools to promote social hygiene and welfare makes sense, if for no other reason, because on any weekday schools are where all the children are supposed to be. No educator of wisdom doubts the value of school nutrition programs, vaccinations, dental and optical examinations, physical education classes, and some extracurricular activities. But generally the peripheral—and political—functions of schools have become so numerous, complicated, and burdensome that they blur and overpower an academic mission.

In this, educational modernists have brought on their own problems. For generations they have expanded the educational apparatus to serve what they have called the "whole child." In doing so, they have sought to turn much of the work of public education into the proper work of parents, social workers, psychologists, police, probation officers, and hospital staffs. Too eagerly they have taken on new and distracting duties to care for every unfortunate and antisocial child, increasingly acting as flunkies and surrogates for self-absorbed, overburdened, or negligent parents. In the suburbs schools have become the training grounds for automobile drivers. In the cities schools have added parenting and family planning classes for expectant and unwed mothers. They have wandered into the territory of moral and sex education, often making such subjects highly controversial by advocating ethical relativism and tolerating sexual permissiveness.

Not only has all of this adulterated the "first curriculum." In a large number of schools nonacademic factions are in control of institutional planning. Perhaps a majority of educational practitioners now conceive of themselves as therapists and social scientists instead of scholars. These instructors are ever eager to take on custodial and nurturing tasks but decidedly cool toward calls for academic renewal. They perceive all reluctant or hostile students as disabled, disturbed, or victimized. Some boldly view the school as an arena where one or another group should be compensated for unequal status or opportunities elsewhere. They allow the principle of compensation to override the principle of institutional quality. Powerful vocational congeries,

177

meanwhile, are interested solely in advancing technical and so-called career skills that schools can then deliver prepackaged to trades. When schools are failing today, no doubt part of the reason is their excessively ambitious and confused mission.

In taking on new caretaking, redemptive, and occupational activities, many in schools have forgotten the schools' primary duty to educate the young. They have forgotten that other social institutions share responsibility for nurturing children, that ignorance and unemployment aggravate psychological maladjustment, that equal educational access means foremost equal academic access, that the best vocational education is in basic subjects and skills that prepare students for rapid on-the-job training. The road to excellence begins where schools decide to curtail the manifold operations that now obstruct or degrade the orderly transmission of general knowledge.

Yet these foregoing reform principles are not enough. Improvements in elementary and secondary schooling depend on concerted local strategies whereby educators in schools and districts act with dispatch and common sense to affirm the idea of educational quality for all children. They also depend on a cultural ethos that values people of lucidity, skill, and discipline. The future of our democratic state demands the presence of broadly held general knowledge, respect for the work ethic, warm and loving elementary teachers and parents, intellectually and vocationally proud secondary instructors, and above all communities with sufficient conviction to direct the educational enterprise toward these ends.

Qualitative school reform cannot and should not be left solely to professional educators. It requires constant agitation on the part of civic leaders, service clubs, employers, and clergy. Corporate managers and labor union officials should realize their mutual benefit in a well-educated labor force. Political leaders of all persuasions should see that in at least one way the quest for educational excellence transcends ideology: It seeks a style of schooling most likely to produce individuals who, for all their variations, can survive and think, contribute to the welfare of the polity, and engage in lifelong individuation.

Most of all, perhaps, the future quality of U.S. schooling depends

178

on the moods of the nation's reigning cultural mandarins and idea brokers. In light of failing liberal nostrums, opinion makers in government, the universities, foundations, and major news outlets must reconsider some ill-advised notions of compassion and justice. Some leading intellectuals must risk their reputations to affirm tradition, the value of mental refinement, and the concept of an overarching social order. They must articulate the means to achieve and enforce narrower perimeters of schoolhouse freedom and service, celebrating the school as a center of learning and character development. School reform cannot occur as long as fashionable people view value moorings like the Boy Scout Code as socially retrograde or obsolete and believe that they are contributing to the social good by denigrating such moorings.

Meaningful school improvement may be possible only within the broader context of a cultural revolution, one that gives more respect to traditional values. At minimum it demands public appreciation of reason and discipline. A critical mass of educators, community leaders, and opinion makers must have the will to face down obsessive paraeducational forces in schools, each pursuing a special interest at the expense of academic standards. So far we have the knowledge to make radical school improvements. What is not quite yet in place is a firm political consensus that values universal learning, hard work, and willingness to sacrifice for the common good.

One can argue, persuasively, that the coming decade will be marked by harrowing and relentless social fragmentation. Perhaps differences between effective public and private schools and schools incapable of educating children will intensify. But then, perhaps not. Renewed interest in traditional forms of education has contributed already to isolated signs of improved school performance, notably in some metropolitan areas. Private and public alternatives are not always convenient, feasible, or, in places, even available. Most public school people (if not national education leaders) are far more receptive to pressure from parents and communities than their reputations would indicate. Since a portion of the education leadership has grown penitent about its recent adventures, the times may be ripe for reform.

It is possible that the determination of some educators to regain the attention, trust, and support of their constituencies will result in seedbeds of excellence that other communities, and more communities after that, will try to replicate. Then a basic academic curriculum in many local forms would provide a common educational backbone for students of all backgrounds and capabilities along with emphasis on orderly learning, high expectations, structured teaching, proficiency requirements, achievement ranking, classroom and schoolyard stability, and ultimately, high cognitive and behavioral outcomes for all children. Such emphases in themselves would not only constitute a dramatic set of educational innovations. If sustained, they would provide a continuing megavitamin program for the social anemia that we have been told, for too long, schools can combat only through nonacademic programs and therapeutic interventions.

The American children born today will come into adulthood at the dawn of a new millenium. The scope and depth of the general knowledge they hold will depend much on how adults in the eighties choose to construe education's meaning. As adults, we have an urgent responsibility to give more to the schools and expect more from them in return. If anti-intellectualism and value neutrality remain prevailing cultural impulses in the coming decade, it is these children on whom our lack of standards, unsound emotional bearings, and failed nerve will ultimately and crushingly fall.

References

Chapter One   A Report Card

There are too few up-to-date surveys of the contemporary elementary and secondary school. The huge literature of the late sixties and early seventies has gathered cobwebs. Even Charles E. Silberman's *Crisis in the Classroom* (Random House, 1970) now seems more like a document of a departed epoch than a useful guide to the terrain of the future. One impressive catalog of conditions in and views toward schools is Torsten Husén's *The School in Question* (Oxford, 1979), especially useful because it records (cold comfort) the presence of similar turmoil and debate about schools in advanced industrial nations besides the United States.

A number of important new essays on conditions in education do exist, beginning with two special serial issues, the first, "Recess Is Over," *The New Republic,* April 18, 1981, and the second, "America's Schools: Public and Private," *Daedalus,* Summer 1981. Four exceptional articles are Diane Divoky, "A Loss of Nerve," *The Wilson Quarterly,* Autumn 1979; Tommy M. Tomlinson, "The Troubled Years: An Interpretive Analysis of Public Schooling since 1950," *Phi Delta Kappan,* January 1981; Joseph Adelson, "What Happened to the Schools," *Commentary,* March 1981; and Diane

Ravitch, "Forgetting the Questions: The Problem of Educational Reform," *The American Scholar,* Summer 1981.

For data on academic productivity I have relied mainly on the ongoing assessments of the National Assessment of Educational Progress in reading, writing, mathematics, science, and civics, reported in NAEP bulletins issued between 1970 and 1982. Annegret Harnischfeger and David E. Wiley, *Achievement Test Score Decline: Do We Need To Worry?* (CEMREL, 1975), provides a composite of national testing trends in the late sixties and early seventies. The downward slide is confirmed in Barbara Lerner's admirable review, "American Education: How Are We Doing?" *The Public Interest,* Fall 1982. For community perceptions of schools, see the annual *Gallup Poll of the Public's Attitudes Toward the Public School,* published each September by *Phi Delta Kappan.*

Violent Schools—Safe Schools: The Safe School Study Report to Congress (National Institute of Education, 1978) is an ambitious and detailed report on crime in public schools during the mid-seventies. (It does not deal with self-destructive "victimless" crimes.) I was aided mightily by Jackson Toby's clearheaded analysis of that report, "Crime in American Public Schools," *The Public Interest,* Winter 1979.

Chester E. Finn, Jr.,'s seminal essays on policy and shifting ideologies in U.S. education should be required reading for any serious observer of today's school. They include "The Future of Education's Liberal Consensus," *Change,* September 1980, and "Toward a New Consensus," *Change,* September 1981.

See Denis P. Doyle's "A Din of Inequity: Private Schools Reconsidered," *Teachers College Record,* Summer 1981. The Gallup Poll of private education and tax credits was conducted in March 1981 and published in *Newsweek,* April 20, 1981.

Chapter Two   The Progressive Century

Two indispensable histories of the social and theoretical forces at work in the development of the American school between 1900 and 1960 are Lawrence Cremin, *The Transformation of the School* (Knopf, 1961), and Richard Hofstadter, *Anti-Intellectualism in American Life* (Knopf, 1963). In their analyses the Columbia colleagues and friends disagreed. Cremin's view of the Progressive movement is far more sanguine than Hofstadter's. After twenty years, however, these two fine books—from which I have borrowed shamelessly—

seem more to complement than to contradict one another. Cremin's essay "Some Problems in the Progressive Theory of Education," a chapter in his *Public Education* (Basic, 1976), includes wise and sophisticated observations about progressive education's history. A very readable, intelligent, and not out-of-date review of schooling is Martin Mayer, *The Schools* (Harper & Brothers, 1961).

To get a firm grasp of Dewey's educational outlook, the place to begin is *Dewey on Education* (Teachers College, 1959), which includes Martin S. Dworkin's excellent introductory essay, "John Dewey: A Centennial Review." In Dworkin's collection, first read Dewey's "My Pedagogic Creed" (1897), Dewey at his most noble, evangelical, and visionary. Dewey's most concise statement on education, written late in his life, partly in protest at the general misapprehension of Deweyan school theories, is *Experience and Education* (Macmillan, 1938). An reconsideration of Dewey may be found in Joseph Featherstone's "John Dewey," *The New Republic,* July 8, 1972.

The vast Deweyan literature of the twenties and thirties first articulates the educational methods so beloved of recent romantics and libertarians, especially in the realms of student freedom, initiative, and activity. At its best it is delightful for its childlike faith in the new education's future. For the most complete account of the Deweyan school ideal of the twenties, there is Harold Rugg and Ann Shumaker, *The Child-Centered School* (World Book, 1928). The book may be read as the definitive polemic of the early Progressives on the proper operations and aims of the elementary school. See also *Cardinal Principles of Secondary Education* (U.S. Government Printing Office, 1918), the revolutionary manifesto calling for nonacademic missions in the nation's high schools.

William H. Kilpatrick's influential writing on progressive education includes "The Project Method," *Teachers College Record,* September 1918, and a fascinating textbook, *Foundations of Method* (Macmillan, 1926). Written in a pretentious Socratic style, the latter is a clear summary of his educational outlook. Samuel Tenenbaum's authorized biography, *William Heard Kilpatrick* (Harper, 1951), is sheer hagiography, though useful for its approving citations of Kilpatrick's many anti-intellectual statements.

George S. Counts, *Dare the School Build a New Social Order?* (Southern Illinois, 1932), sounded the ideological siren for the thirties. His votary Theodore Brameld tried to develop a full theory of reconstructionism in *Patterns of Educational Philosophy* (World Book, 1950).

Boyd H. Bode's major contributions to the education debate came in *Modern Educational Theories* (Macmillan, 1927) and *Progressive Education at the Crossroads* (Newson, 1938). Another lucid and valuable Bode essay is "The Confusion in Present-Day Education," which appears in *The Educational Frontier* (Appleton-Century, 1933).

William C. Bagley is perhaps the most ignored of the major educational philosophers of the century, presumably shunned because of his deviation from Deweyan enthusiasms of the thirties. Even Cremin's history all but excludes him. Bagley's theory of Essentialism was developed through a number of articles. To understand the subject-centered view, read "Is Subject-Matter Obsolete?" *Educational Administration and Supervision,* September 1935; his Essentialist manifesto, "An Essentialist's Platform for the Advancement of Education," *Educational Administration and Supervision,* April 1938; "The Significance of the Essentialist Movement in Educational Theory," *The Classical Journal,* 34 (1938–39); and his summary, "Just What Is the Crux of the Conflict between the Progressives and the Essentialists?" *Educational Administration and Supervision,* 26 (1940). I. L. Kandel's biography, *William Chandler Bagley* (Teachers College, 1961), is of high quality.

Essentialist attacks at mid-century included Arthur Bestor's *Educational Wastelands* (Illinois, 1953) and his more comprehensive *The Restoration of Learning* (Knopf, 1955). By comparison, Mortimer Smith's *And Madly Teach* (Regnery, 1949) and *The Diminished Mind* (Regnery, 1954) are dated and shrill diatribes. John F. Latimer attempted to quantify the declining academic standards of the twentieth-century secondary school in *What Happened to Our High Schools* (Public Affairs Press, 1958). An accessible and level-headed critique of the mid-century progressive school is Paul Woodring's *Let's Talk Sense About Our Schools* (McGraw-Hill, 1953), a book at once sympathetic to progressive education and upset by its excesses. Two key works by anti-Progressives outside the Bestor camp are Robert M. Hutchins, *The Conflict in Education in a Democratic Society* (Harper & Brothers, 1953), and Hyman G. Rickover, *Education and Freedom* (Dutton, 1959). James B. Conant's consensus response was *The American High School Today* (McGraw-Hill, 1959).

Chapter Three   The Era of Equality and Ecstasy

A fine introduction to the politics and place of education in the Great Society's reform program may be found in "No Crystal Stair," a chapter in Godfrey Hodgson's *America in Our Time* (Random House, 1976). A group of high-quality essays reconsidering *Brown* v. *Topeka*'s impact since the fifties are collected in Derrick Bell, ed., *Shades of Brown: New Perspectives on School*

Desegregation (Teachers College, 1980). In *ESEA: The Office of Education Administers a Law* (Syracuse, 1968), Stephen K. Bailey and Edith K. Mosher give a detailed account of the politics of the Elementary and Secondary Education Act, noting that its ends were less the search for educationally sound ways of raising achievement levels, and more the conclusion of a frustrating battle by liberals to engineer increased federal aid to schools. Mortimer Smith's observations on ESEA were published in *A Decade of Comment on Education 1956–1966* (Council for Basic Education, 1966) under the heading "Federal Aid."

The Coleman Report was published as James S. Coleman et al., *Equality of Economic Opportunity* (U.S. Government Printing Office, 1966). Coleman himself evaluated the significance of his report in "Equal Schools or Equal Students?" *The Public Interest,* Summer 1966. A perceptive early review of the Coleman report and its implications for education's future is Daniel P. Moynihan's March 1967 address, "The Education of the Urban Poor," later printed in *Coping: Essays on the Practice of Government* (Random House, 1973). The Jencks report was published as Christopher Jencks et al., *Inequality: A Reassessment of the Effect of Family and Schooling in America* (Basic, 1972). One acute review of the study is Melville J. Ulmer's "Does Schooling Matter?" *The New Republic,* November 18, 1972. In light of rampant egalitarianism during the early seventies, Charles Frankel wrote an essay called "The New Egalitarianism and the Old," *Commentary,* September 1973, still timely a decade later.

Sample revisionist histories of American schooling are, in chronological order: Michael B. Katz, *Class, Bureaucracy and Schools* (Praeger, 1971); Samuel Bowles and Herbert Gintis, *Schooling in Capitalist America* (Basic, 1976); and David Nasaw, *Schooled to Order* (Oxford, 1979). At the invitation of the National Academy of Education, Diane Ravitch reviewed the works of the radical historians as a group, which resulted in her *The Revisionists Revised* (Basic, 1978). The book, because it broke with then trendy historiography, received less favorable criticism than it deserved. The debate over the nature of the educational past continues with Walter Feinberg's and colleagues' weak rejoinder, *Revisionists Respond to Ravitch* (National Academy of Education, 1980).

Chapter Four   The Perils of Benevolence

Those interested in reviewing federal and state educational policies during the seventies and early eighties may want to turn first to *Debating National*

Education Policy: A Question of Standards (American Enterprise Institute, 1981), a useful handbook compiled by the school analyst Denis P. Doyle. A trenchant and liberal critique of many of these policies is to be found in Arthur E. Wise, *Legislated Learning* (California, 1979). See also Robert A. Miller, ed., *The Federal Role in Education: New Directions for the Eighties* (Institute for Educational Leadership, 1981), a collection of essays reviewing federal policy as it has evolved since ESEA. It includes worthy recommendations for policy reform in the eighties, though specific pieces vary in quality. The article by Samuel Halperin, "Education Policy for the Eighties: We Can't Get There From Here," is a good place to start. For better understanding of federal–local relations, go to Eleanor Farrar et al., "Views from Below: Implementation Research in Education," *Teachers College Record,* Fall 1980.

The literature of Washington-driven educational policy and policy-making is vast. I have listed below only a few works that I have found especially useful or instructive.

DESEGREGATION

The opinions that demonstrate the Supreme Court's line of reasoning in abandoning *Brown* v. *Topeka*'s principle of color-blindness in pupil school assignments are collected in *Selected Court Decisions Relating to Equal Educational Opportunity* (U.S. Government Printing Office, 1972). An essay arguing against the wisdom—and constitutionality—of these decisions is Nathan Glazer's "Is Busing Necessary?" *Commentary,* March 1972. An acid and more extensive review of these decisions is contained in Lino A. Graglia, *Disaster by Decree* (Cornell, 1976).

David J. Armor's early report on busing, "Evidence on Busing," *The Public Interest,* Summer 1972, aroused intense controversy, since Armor had amassed impressive early evidence to indicate that forced integration procedures were not working. A second wave of controversy resulted from James S. Coleman's allegation of connection between busing and white flight. His charge was made first at a meeting of the American Educational Research Association in April 1975, receiving sufficient publicity to be followed by a federally funded "Symposium on School Desegregation and White Flight" held at the Brookings Institution in August. Some desegregation specialists have argued against the existence of white flight. An influential article *contra* Coleman was Christine H. Rossell, "School Desegregation and White Flight," *Political Science Quarterly,* Winter 1975–76. Diane Ravitch challenged Rossell and others in "The 'White Flight' Controversy," *The Public Interest,*

Spring 1978. Rossell and Ravitch (along with David J. Armor) continued the debate in "Busing and 'White Flight,'" *The Public Interest,* Fall 1978. The Armor quotation is from his essay "Unwillingly to School," *Policy Review,* Fall 1981. The chief proponent for more aggressive desegregation efforts is Willis D. Hawley of Vanderbilt University, who directed a seven-year National Institute of Education study. It was published in 1981 as the nine-volume *Assessment of Current Knowledge about the Effectiveness of School Desegregation Strategies,* available from Vanderbilt's Institute for Public Policy Studies.

COMPENSATORY EDUCATION

The liabilities of Title I are best considered in Paul Copperman, *The Literacy Hoax* (Morrow, 1978), and in Harriet T. Bernstein and Daniel W. Merenda, "Categorical Programs: Past and Present," in Miller, ed., *The Federal Role in Education,* cited above.

BILINGUAL EDUCATION

See Noel Epstein, *Language, Ethnicity, and the School* (Institute for Educational Leadership, 1977), and Tom Bethell's stinging "Against Bilingual Education," *Harper's,* February 1979. The first major report to suggest bilingual education's ill effects was the American Institutes for Research, *Interim Report: Evaluation of the Impact of ESEA Title VII Spanish/English Bilingual Education Programs,* February 1977. The second report was prepared for the Department of Education's Office of Planning, Budget, and Evaluation and made public by *The Washington Post* in 1981, shortly after the newspaper obtained drafts through the Freedom of Information Act.

An evenhanded but negative review of bilingual education may also be found in Iris C. Rotberg, "Some Legal and Research Considerations in Establishing Federal Policy in Bilingual Education," *Harvard Educational Review,* May 1982. A standard work on bilingual education, and very biased in its favor, is Francesco Cordaseo, *Bilingual Schooling in the United States* (McGraw-Hill, 1976). I have drawn the Saginaw, Michigan, example from Gene I. Maeroff's *Don't Blame the Kids* (McGraw-Hill, 1981), a readable book containing many graphic anecdotes of unintended side effects of recent public policy.

EDUCATION OF THE HANDICAPPED

Two noteworthy articles on the mandates in force on the educational rights of the handicapped are Maynard C. Reynolds, "Education of the Handicapped: Some Areas of Confusion," *Phi Delta Kappan,* May 1980, and an even more impressive piece, John C. Pittenger and Peter Kuriloff, "Educating the Handicapped: Reforming a Radical Law," *The Public Interest,* Winter 1982.

STUDENT RIGHTS

Tinker and other cases are summarized and analyzed in Robert H. Mnookin, *Child, Family, and State: Problems and Materials on Children and the Law* (Little, Brown, 1978). With the expressed purpose of showing students how to protect their legal rights, and showing exceeding hostility to *in loco parentis,* the American Civil Liberties Union published a handbook, *The Rights of Students* (Avon, 1973), edited by Alan H. Levine et al. Leon Letwin's analysis of student rights is to be found in "After Goss V. Lopez: Student Status as Suspect Classification?" 29 *Stanford Law Review* 627 (1977). A more extreme advocacy of student rights and youth emancipation may be found in an alarming collection of essays, *The Children's Rights Movement: Overcoming the Oppression of Young People* (Anchor, 1977), edited by Beatrice and Ronald Gross.

TESTING

I have drawn a good deal of material from my own coverage of the antitesting movement that peaked in 1979 and 1980. For background see George Weber, *Uses and Abuses of Standardized Testing in the Schools* (Council for Basic Education, 1974), and Christopher Jencks and James Crouse, "Aptitude vs. Achievement: Should We Replace the SAT?" *The Public Interest,* Spring 1982. An intelligent review of the SAT is to be found in Jay Amberg, "The SAT," *The American Scholar,* Autumn 1982. To date, from the National Academy of Sciences, the most authoritative analytical review of a variety of tests used in schools is Alexandra K. Wigdor and Wendell R. Garner, eds., *Ability Testing: Uses, Consequences, and Controversies,* 2 vols. (National Academy Press, 1982).

THE RISE OF THE SPECIAL INTERESTS

Two admirable essays describe the politicization of the NEA: Robert W. Kagan, "A Relic of the New Age: The National Education Association," *The American Spectator,* February 1982, and Chester E. Finn, Jr., "Teacher Politics," *Commentary,* February 1983.

Chapter Five   The Changing World of Childhood

This pessimistic chapter rests in part on disturbing observations made in several cultural surveys, notably Robert Nisbet, *The Twilight of Authority* (Oxford, 1975); Daniel Bell, *The Cultural Contradictions of Capitalism* (Basic, 1976); and Christopher Lasch, *The Culture of Narcissism* (Norton, 1978). I am also indebted to Joseph Adelson's brilliant overview of schooling, "What Happened to the Schools," cited in the Chapter One section, which I quote from here. A review of atomizing forces in U.S. society at large can be found in Kevin Phillips, "The Balkanization of America," *Harper's,* May 1978. Paul Copperman, *The Literary Hoax,* cited in the previous section, contains a splendid chapter on the abdication of adult authority and its impact on schoolhouse disorder. A classic treatment of the relationship between authority and education is R. S. Peters, *Authority, Responsibility and Education* (George Allen & Unwin, 1973). The complicated theme of authority is at the center, too, of Gerald Grant's penetrating essay "The Character of Education and the Education of Character," *Daedalus,* Summer 1981.

The composite table of changing influences on adolescents first appeared in Alonzo A. Crim, "A Community of Believers," *Daedalus,* Fall 1981. Data on family conditions are derived largely from Department of Health and Human Services and U.S. Census collections. The special problems of the welfare household are treated in Morley D. Glicken, "Transgenerational Welfare Dependency," *Journal of Contemporary Studies,* Summer 1981, and in Martin Kilson, "Black Social Classes and Intergenerational Poverty," *The Public Interest,* Summer 1981. Arlene Skolnick collects the revised view of family life and makes the case for emancipated childhood in her anthology *Rethinking Childhood* (Little, Brown, 1976). For comparison see Mary Jo Bane, *Here to Stay: American Families in the Twentieth Century* (Basic, 1976). On the heritage and value of organized religion in the United States, I have referred to Terry Eastland, "In Defense of Religious America," *Commentary,* June 1981.

The power of the adolescent peer group is carefully explained in James

191

S. Coleman's seminal *The Adolescent Society* (Free Press, 1961). The topic is analyzed more freshly in Christopher Lasch, *Haven in a Heartless World* (Basic, 1977). In this book Lasch reviews earlier sociological commentary on peer groups, finds it wanting, and proceeds to set out some cogent explanations for faulty relations between adults and children today.

There is, of course, a vast and contradictory literature on television's function as an educative instrument. Overall, George Comstock's writings on the subject remain most impressive. A good summary of his analyses is to be found in "Television Entertainment: Taking It Seriously," *Character,* October 1980. See his *Television in America* (Sage, 1980) for more details. George Comstock et al., *Television and Human Behavior* (Columbia, 1978), is definitive. Other research of merit on the subject of television comes from the prolific pens of Dorothy G. Singer and Jerome L. Singer; *Television, Imagination and Aggression* (Erlbaum, 1981) is their most recent effort. The California survey on educational achievement and television was first reported in the 1979–80 annual report of the California Assessment Program, a spinoff of NAEP. See also Neil Postman's persuasive essay *The Disappearance of Childhood* (Delacorte, 1982). I observed firsthand the relentless and reflexive modernism of some television producers and screenwriters—with some humor and more alarm—at the 1981 Aspen Institute conference on "Images of Adolescence." On Hollywood's gaudy view of America, see Ben Stein's delightful *The View from Sunset Boulevard* (Basic, 1979).

There is no shortage of scholarly and popular writing on juvenile alienation. Most of it assumes or seeks to prove that increasing individual freedom is the best remedy. Thus it is not useful. Robert Nisbet's remarks on boredom are to be found in *History of the Idea of Progress* (Basic, 1980). Data on juvenile drug use come from my own composite of surveys published through 1982 by the National Institute on Drug Abuse and *The New York Times,* as well as the findings of a large and reliable 1981 high school survey in Riverside County, California. The statistics on teenage sexual activity and pregnancy are from a 1979 survey conducted by the Johns Hopkins School of Hygiene and Public Health and from a 1981 report of the Alan Guttmacher Institute.

Chapter Six The Common School in Crisis

Much of this chapter is based on my own visits to schools and school districts in 1981 and 1982. I have also relied on *The New York Time's* coverage during the same time of trends in school structure, educational finance, population change, residential movement, and private school participation. Coleman's remarks on the possibilities for the common school appear in his essay "Quality and Equality in American Education," *Phi Delta Kappan,* November 1981. There exist few candid treatments of racial policies in elementary and secondary schools. For an account of the shocking inequalities that low-income minorities face on account of skewed notions of compensation, compassion, and justice, read Fred Reed's excellent essay, "The Color of Education," *Harper's,* February 1981.

Grant's quotation on private education comes from "The Character of Education and the Education of Character," *Daedalus,* cited above. Doyle's and Vitullo-Martin's remarks are from Denis P. Doyle, "A Din of Inequity: Private Schools Reconsidered," also cited. The fairest treatment of Christian schools, that is, an analysis sophisticated enough to treat racial *and* nonracial motives in the movement, is Peter Skerry, "Christian Schools Versus the I.R.S.," *The Public Interest,* Fall 1980. The Skerry article is useful, too, in describing federal hostility to private education at the end of the seventies. A more skeptical view of Christian schools may be found in David Nevin and Robert E. Bills, *The Schools That Fear Built* (Acropolis, 1976). The data on inner-city parochial schools come from a preliminary report conducted by the Catholic League for Religious and Civil Rights under the leadership of the Reverend Virgil C. Blum, presented at a 1980 conference of the National Catholic Education Association. The preliminary findings of the Coleman study of private schools come from "Summary of Major Findings for Public and Private Schools," by James Coleman, Thomas Hoffer, and Sally Kilgore, issued in March 1981. This was one early analysis of the *High School and Beyond* study, commissioned by the National Center for Education Statistics and based on the most extensive collection of data ever compiled about American high school students. The Coleman analysis later appeared in finished form as James S. Coleman et al., *High School Achievement* (Basic, 1982).

Chapter Seven   Turning Toward Basics

The first articles identifying a back-to-basics trend appeared in education trade magazines and the popular press in 1974. Diane Divoky apparently coined the term "back-to-basics" in her article "Opting for the Old-Fangled Alternative," *Learning,* February 1974. An early treatment of the movement was Suzanne de Lesseps's "Education's Return to Basics," Editorial Research Reports, *Congressional Quarterly,* September 1975. In March 1977 *Phi Delta Kappan* magazine carried a balanced suite of articles on back-to-basics. The school boards survey and other useful statements on basics, pro and con, may be found in *Back-to-Basics,* National School Boards Association, Research Report 1978–1. The monthly bulletin of the Council for Basic Education deals topically with school trends as seen through the Essentialist filter.

An early report on the minimum competency testing drive is Shirley Boes Neill, *The Competency Movement, Problems and Solutions* (American Association of School Administrators, 1978). See also Joseph Beckham, *Legal Implications of Minimum Competency Testing* (Phi Delta Kappa, 1980), and Dennis Gray, *Minimum Competency Testing* (Council for Basic Education, 1980). The Research and Information Department of the Education Commission of the States prepares frequent state-by-state summaries of ongoing competency legislation, rulings by state boards of education, and testing activities by state departments of education.

Henry S. Myers's disappointing tract on John Marshall Fundamental School in particular and back-to-basics schools in general is *Fundamentally Speaking* (Strawberry Hill, 1977).

The Wingspread conference is reported in Ben Brodinsky, "Defining the Basics in American Education" (Phi Delta Kappa, 1977), reprinted in part in the NSBA report cited above. Christopher Jencks's intelligent critique of back-to-basics appeared as "The Wrong Answer for Schools Is: (b) Back to Basics" in *The Washington Post,* February 19,1978.

Chapter Eight   What Makes an Effective School

Perhaps the most amazing thing about the school effectiveness research that has appeared in sundry reports, technical journals, and educational trade publications is the limited public attention it has received. (The 1981 Coleman report proves the rule by exception.) The emerging synthesis on what makes for superior schools, sadly, is not at all well known even to school board members, superintendents, principals, and teachers. In order to invigorate the education debate of the eighties, what is needed in the coming years is further commentary, review, and editorial statement on the qualitative issues raised by the following scholarly efforts.

The three pioneering studies on school effectiveness are George Weber, *Inner-City Children Can Be Taught to Read: Four Successful Schools* (Council for Basic Education, 1971); Neville Bennett et al., *Teaching Styles and Pupil Progress* (Harvard, 1976); and Michael Rutter et al., *Fifteen Thousand Hours: Secondary Schools and Their Effects on Children* (Harvard, 1979). For an appraisal of the implications of the Rutter report and the state of conventional thinking about schools at the end of the seventies, see Gerald Grant's review of *Fifteen Thousand Hours* in *The New Republic,* June 16, 1979.

No U.S. study on the properties of effective schools matches Rutter's work for fastidiousness. Some scholarship, especially the work of Ronald Edmonds, has been called into question for a lack of adequate data base. Several researchers and journalists have faulted James S. Coleman's methodology. The weaknesses and simplicities in some school effectiveness research are documented in Stewart C. Purkey and Marshall S. Smith, *Effective Schools: A Review* (National Institute of Education, 1982). Still, the accumulation of similar conclusions by a flock of fair-minded and competent scholars is impressive. I have drawn my own synthesis on effective urban schools with assistance from the following works and reports: Michael Cohen, "Effective Schools: Accumulating Research Findings," *American Education,* January–February 1982; W. B. Brookover et al., *School Social Systems and Student Achievement: Schools Can Make a Difference* (Praeger, 1979); Jere E. Brophy, "Teacher Behavior and Student Learning," *Educational Leadership,* October 1979, and "Successful Teaching Strategies for the Inner-City Child," *Phi Delta Kappan,* April 1982; and Ronald Edmonds, "Effective Schools for the Urban Poor," *Educational Leadership,* October 1979. See also Robert Benjamin's accessible *Making Schools Work* (Continuum, 1981), a descriptive review of some exceptionally successful inner-city schools.

On Coleman II, I have again used the preliminary summary and finished report, *High School Achievement,* each cited above. Coleman himself reviewed the meaning of his study in "Private Schools, Public Schools, and the Public Interest," *The Public Interest,* Summer 1981, and, with Hoffer and Kilgore, tried to answer critics in *Harvard Educational Review,* Fall 1981. Diane Ravitch also inspected the report's significance in "The Meaning of the New Coleman Report," *Phi Delta Kappan,* June 1981, and in "What Makes a Good School?" *Society,* January–February 1982. In the same issue of *Society,* Coleman and his assistants once again interpreted their findings and explained why they had reached certain policy conclusions. Robert L. Crain and Willis D. Hawley responded here by attacking Coleman's research standards and the reliability of the report.

In considering schools as nurseries of virtue, I return again and again to sections of Plato's *Republic* and Aristotle's *Politics.* In a wiser world such philosophical works, not accreted court opinions, might provide the basic ethical armament for schools. The best recent analytical treatment of school climates is Gerald Grant's elegant essay "The Character of Education and the Education of Character," cited in the Chapter Six section. I have also used Edward A. Wynne's impressionistic and personal *Looking at Schools: Good, Bad and Indifferent* (Lexington, 1980).

As noted in the text, several prescriptive reports, particularly directed at secondary school reform, are scheduled to appear in 1983 and 1984. One dramatic manifesto has already appeared to wide—and mixed—reviews: Mortimer J. Adler et al., *The Paideia Proposal* (Macmillan, 1982). Controversies over Adler's statements have revolved around practicality. Consequently the Paideia Group now promises a second volume addressing the problems of implementing a universal one-track course of study. Also see the report of the National Commission on Excellence in Education, *A Nation At Risk* (U.S. Government Printing Office, 1983).

Chapter Nine   Reform and Its Barriers

The Modesto Plan is outlined in James C. Enochs, *The Restoration of Standards: The Modesto Plan* (Phi Delta Kappa, 1979), and described in Robert C. Benjamin, *Making Schools Work,* cited in the preceding section.

In making the case for smaller (and presumably more diversified) schools, especially at the secondary level, I have been influenced by the studies summarized in the ERIC Clearinghouse on Educational Management report, "School Size," January 1982.

Arthur E. Wise's remarks on career education are to be found in *Legislated Learning,* cited in the Chapter Four section.

In analyzing the condition of teachers and the teaching profession, I have relied especially on ongoing Gallup reports; W. Timothy Weaver, "In Search of Quality: The Need for Talent in Teaching," *Phi Delta Kappan,* September 1979; and J. Myron Atkin, "Who Will Teach in High School?" *Daedalus,* Summer 1981. Dan C. Lortie provides the fullest sociological portrait extant of contemporary instructors in *Schoolteacher* (Chicago, 1975). See also Richard A. Hawley's sensitive writing on the substance of teaching, notably "Teaching as Failing," *Phi Delta Kappan,* April 1979, and "Mr. Chips Redux," *The Atlantic,* November 1980. For review of chief union concerns and initiatives see Lorraine McDonnell and Anthony Pascal, *Organized Teachers in American Schools* (National Institute of Education, 1979). In spite of its overly protective stance toward incompetent teachers, the American Federation of Teachers displays an interest in educational standards not shared by the National Education Association. An authoritative review of differences between the AFT and the NEA may be found in Chester E.

Finn, Jr.,'s *Commentary* piece on teachers' politics, cited in the Chapter Four section.

Chapter Ten   The Cultivation of Excellence

A fine recent case for educational excellence is made in Steven M. Cahn, *Education and the Democratic Ideal* (Nelson-Hall, 1979). With grace, wit, and clarity Cahn attempts to reconcile contradictions between excellence and equality, liberty and discipline, individuality and authority. For older definitions of basic and subject-centered education, see Clifton Fadiman's title essay in James D. Koerner, ed., *The Case for Basic Education* (Little, Brown, 1959), and Robert M. Hutchins, *The Conflict in Education in a Democratic Society,* cited in the Chapter Two section. A sophisticated explanation of what basic education means is also contained in Dennis Gray's remarks to the House Subcommittee on Elementary, Secondary, and Vocational Education, February 5, 1980.

In formulating my list of principles, I have been influenced by the sources above, as well as by Chester E. Finn, Jr.,'s paper "High School Reform in the Eighties: Consensus or Cacophony?" (Council for Basic Education, 1981); Peter R. Greer's working paper "Essentials of Quality Education," presented at a conference on effective schools at Columbia University's Teachers College, June 29, 1981; and James C. Enochs's *The Restoration of Standards: The Modesto Plan,* cited in the preceding section.

Index